UP LEVEL
PROJECT

Your Guide to Unlocking Higher Profits While
Creating More Freedom

Pam,

   Thank you for being a VIP!

♡ Hanneke

Hanneke Antonelli

ISBN 978-1-7368550-1-0

Design by Lisa McKenna
Edited by James Reed
Drawing by Daniël Hugo

For more information visit theuplevelprojectbook.com

To my dad, a man of few words,
who taught me to be strong, brave, and tenacious.

Thank you for allowing me to dream big, for sharing in my
love of numbers and business, and for making me realize
I could achieve all the same things that boys do.

TABLE OF CONTENTS:

INTRODUCTION:

"You are the creator of your own reality because
you are the chooser of the thought right now."

–ABRAHAM HICKS

I have to come clean. I, me, the 5-foot-4-ish girl from a small and conservative farming community in South Africa, never thought I'd end up living and running a business in the U.S. And I definitely never fathomed being the author of a book. Let alone did I ever in my wildest dreams imagine that I'd write that book on the topic of entrepreneurship and in my second language.

But the truth is, I wish someone had given me this book when I started my first business. It would have saved me so much time, money, and lots of tears.

Nothing will test you and your beliefs of what is possible more than growing and managing a business.

While running my first business, I thought it was all about the strategy—getting the right marketing plan, generating scalable revenue streams, and doing all.the.things to grow faster and better.

So I read all the books, bought a bunch of online courses, and still felt like I was running in quicksand, sinking fast. Despite following all the strategies to a T, I wasn't getting those glowing results they promised, not even coming close to meeting the high expectations I set for myself.

Like so many other business owners, I interpreted this to mean that I was somehow flawed. So, to compensate, I started to overwork and obsessively searched for that elusive silver-bullet strategy.

My Wall Street experience and the strict ballet and piano modalities I learned as a child taught me how to be disciplined, tenacious, and hustle harder than anyone else.

It felt like I was born to be an entrepreneur (although I had not quite started to view myself as one), and from the outside, it looked like I was successful.

I built two award-winning businesses in less than five years. And yet, like so many other business owners, I was burnt out, frustrated, riddled with fear and doubts, and verging on resentment because I was still struggling to be as profitable as I wanted to be.

I didn't even see my brand as a business. Instead, I thought of it merely as a passion project that also paid me some money. Entrepreneurs were people who were much smarter and creative than I was; surely, I couldn't possibly be one of those fine folks.

That mindset right there was one of the culprits that led to burning everything down and starting my coaching practice. Not showing up and running my brand as the business it had bloomed into, along with the fact that I also didn't view myself as a leader, prohibited me from growing faster.

And over the years, while coaching many multiple six- to seven-figure business owners, it has become apparent that many entrepreneurs step into this booby trap too.

Building a sustainable business has a lot to do with strategy, yes, but it has so much more to do with your mindset than most people realize.

In this book, I'll reveal the Up Level Formula, a tool that not only saved me from the clutches of depression but also helped me and many of my clients grow a sustainable and profitable business. This equation will help you to streamline and achieve your goals.

Although other business books touch on the importance of mindset, I've yet to read one that gives a quick and easy formula about how the mind works. And of the many business and leadership books I've devoured, none of them have ever talked about the most vital shift that needs to happen if you want to scale faster while creating more flexibility.

That critical pivot is this: There's a definitive point in business where you, as the owner, need to move from self-leadership to leading others. You have to become the visionary, CEO, and leader of your company.

All business owners think that to achieve that next level of success and profit, they need to hunt down and implement that elusive business strategy.

The reality is, there are no secret, fancy strategies that you haven't heard about already. At a certain level, you either know what works, or you hire (and lead) rock stars to incorporate those strategies and innovative visions for you.

When you reach this crucial point, there is only one thing that will keep you from attaining the success and freedom you crave: your inner landscape. That entails your self-esteem and how you show up to lead.

Call it whatever you will—your thoughts, your beliefs, your past experiences, and traumas. These have a massive impact on how you run your business and its profit potential.

The strategies you're trying to execute in your business are failing you, or are not giving you those mind-blowing results, because they don't line up with what you believe, think, say, feel, and how you act.

For years, I walked past this statement: "Opportunity lies within."

As in, I literally walked by it. It was chiseled into the wall of a Boys and Girls Club near my house, and it served as a daily reminder that we have the power to create our destiny.

In this book and in the Up Level Program—my accompanying online course that builds on the framework laid out in the coming chapters—I'll give you the tools to create what might seem impossible.

We'll explore your beliefs and how to shift and change them so they can serve you in your pursuit of wealth and fulfillment. I'll give examples from my own experiences, beginning with one devastating event that completely changed the course of my life, and share the experiences of a few clients who were gracious enough to allow me to share their results.

All the events and experiences I share in this book are true. In some places, I've changed the names and specifics of individuals for privacy reasons.

The beauty of it all is that once you apply the exercises that will redirect your perspective, the perfect business strategies for accelerated growth will reveal themselves to you. You'll instinctively be able to spot new opportunities while confidently and decisively leading the way to attain them.

The purpose of this book, and my program, is to show you the infinite power and possibility that lie within you to accomplish anything you want while having more fun, making more money, and working less.

I have personally tested—and benefited from—all of the tools and skills you'll learn. They've also led dozens of entrepreneurs to have breakthroughs and restored their passion for their businesses while upping their profits.

To further help you implement and dive deeper into the exercises I share, I also included a book resource page with bonuses that you can access by signing up at this link: hannekeantonelli.com/book-bonus

After implementing the techniques shared in this book and my Up Level Program, a client said this:

> I increased my clarity and next steps for my business, discovered aspects of my leadership capabilities, and learned techniques to release what was holding me back.

And another said:

> The most dramatic "aha moment" was the necessity for me to lead myself before leading others. My business has been reignited on all levels as a result of my participation in the Up Level Program. I anticipate my team being more proactive and independent.

As entrepreneurs, we often start our businesses with the dream of creating more financial freedom but build prisons for ourselves instead. We are locked up, growing more resentful and less excited about what we strive to achieve every day.

I've written this book to help you unlock, and escape, this jail.

Are you ready to take your place as a confident leader and CEO of your business while creating more success, satisfaction, and freedom?

Then let's begin.

Gaining Clarity

1. The Commitment: Going all in

2. Are you suffocating joy?

3. How to get what you really want

4. What got you here won't get you where you want to go next

CHAPTER 1:

The Commitment: Going all in

I suddenly snap back into my body. My arm's jammed in a door. I'm in a corridor screaming at him to open the door and give me my phone back... And the door keeps being slammed on my arm. I'm angry, crying, screaming, filled with such immense rage and confusion... what in the actual HELL just happened?!

Finally, the door swings open while he's still screaming at me. I'm not really making sense of anything he's saying. I am focused on one thing. Getting my phone. I see it on the kitchen counter, I grab it, and then I'm out of there... He's still screaming at me, something about not understanding the stresses of having a career. I'm not paying any attention to him at all.

My head is exploding with my own inner dialogue: "Get out of here! Hurry, just get yourself out of here!" I'm running; no, this is definitely a sprint. A sprint to get to safety. I am sprinting from all the adrenaline in my body. The same adrenaline that jolted me back to consciousness in his apartment.

It takes me a few seconds to get the security gate outside his house open. Finally, it swings open, and I'm in my car. I'm safe.

How did this all happen?

I look at my little cell phone. It's about 2:30 in the morning. Thank goodness I was able to get in there again and get to my phone.

But what now!?

Think.

My mind starts to replay the evening. There was kissing. There was a bath. Then it goes blank. The next thing I was conscious again, up against a sink, naked and screaming at him to stop. Adrenaline pumping through me. Confused. Violated.

I must know for sure what just happened. Where to now. It takes me a few minutes to start thinking straight again. Bonnie. My friend who's in medical school. I'll call her—she'll know what to do.

About 30 minutes later, we're at the hospital, but they won't do a rape kit without a police report.

The words hit me like a ton of bricks. Cold, foreign, unreal.

How in the actual heck did I just end up here?

Barely 22, and the victim of date rape.

To get to the bottom of this—we have to go back a little further. Age 14, when I first started showing signs of anxiety. My grades jumped almost overnight from an average student to first in my class.

I have a vivid memory of going from a child to a hormone-filled teenager. How? Anxiety. I went from a little girl with no worry in the world to someone who constantly worried.

Fast forward to age 17. I'm a nervous wreck.

I'm standing in the middle of a church about to sing a duet with an opera singer. *Pie Jesu* by Andrew Lloyd Webber, I was singing the boy part.

Still overcoming the shame of my previous blip (where I messed up in the middle of the church at a very la-di-da wedding), my nerves are doubled. Minutes before, my voice teacher had pulled me aside and held me by my shoulders, leaning in, looking me right in the eyes, she said: "you're going to sing nicely today, right?" I know what she's implying, don't mess up again like you did a few weeks ago at that wedding.

My stomach bunches up just a wee bit more ... the performance goes seamlessly until the very last few bars... I miss my key... my teacher turns around and looks up, disappointment all over her face while she shakes her head right to left.

Confirming a nagging fear that has started to take hold inside my being. A fear that is gripping tighter and shooting more roots every day. Ready to sprout as a foundational belief.

It's the belief that completely runs my life.

It's the belief that ensures me that no matter how well I do, it's never good enough.

It's pressuring and demanding that I do better and better, and better still!

It's also this very belief that makes me long for the attention and approval of men and people who don't deserve me.

It's the belief that grips most of us:

I am simply just not good enough.

Have you noticed how it runs you too?

It's always hiding in the shadows of all your biggest hopes and dreams, creating just the right amount of doubt to send chills of fear down your spine. It's also the very thing that prevents you from going for what you truly want.

It's usually that little voice in your head that starts a sentence with: "What if?"

What if you don't have what it takes?!

Which usually sends your mind into a counter-argument marathon that lasts for hours or sometimes even days.

In very severe cases, you might avoid being alone because that's when this little belief hits the hardest. This is when your anxiety shoots through the roof. That's why you stay so busy. You fill your every moment with something to do, people to see. The thought of being or sitting still by yourself makes you anxious.

This is exactly where my head's at the very second after I finish that duet in church.

I want the earth to swallow me whole; I don't know what else happens in the sermon; I just want to get out and get home to the safety of my room. Odd, I know because that means I'll be alone with all my self-loathing thoughts. The very ones I've tried to push away.

Finally, the sermon is over. I run home with tears streaming down my face. Storming into the house, slamming my door. Ugly, loud sobbing.

The thoughts:

I suck

I'm an idiot

I'm not good enough

Runs on repeat in my head.

A few weeks later, I see my first therapist, and I'm diagnosed with depression.

I'm a combination of mortified and overwhelmed. I've already branded myself as somewhat of an outcast, being a nerd, and being in boarding school. Which today, of course, I can clearly see as the depression taking its hold on me, trying to make me feel separate from everything and everyone. Depression is a smart disease. It knows exactly how to work you over so that it can keep thriving and keep getting a better hold of you. It messes with your self-esteem, which makes you not want to socialize or share with people. Which isolates you more, which keeps feeding the beast.

I see the therapist about three more times, get put on antidepressants, and life goes on.

My anxiety improves, but those thoughts of not being enough continue.

And the worst of my depression is yet to come.

A few years later—almost exactly a year before the rape incident—I'm admitted to hospital and put on suicide watch after my antidepressant medicine malfunctions.

Turns out that I was in that small percentage of people whose antidepressants stopped working over time. Doctors can't quite explain why this happens.[1] But I'm pretty sure my student lifestyle of too little sleep, a diet that wasn't the greatest, with a touch of too much booze wasn't helping.

My psychologist who I'd been seeing weekly for a month or so, refers me to a psychiatrist to get me on new antidepressants.

It's one week in on the new medicine that I hit true rock bottom. I'd been crying the entire week. I couldn't get out of bed, or even leave my room. The meds they prescribed weren't the right dosage or combination for me. And as a result, my depression had intensified. Its claws firmly clutched around my neck, silently suffocating me. I was in the deepest, darkest place I can ever recall. I had thoughts about killing myself running through my head constantly. "I'll walk in front of a bus—that should do it."

It's at this point that the psychiatrist suggested that I be admitted to hospital so they could adjust my medicine under supervision.

I was living in an apartment off-campus at university, two hours away from my parents. So I asked a friend to drop me off at the hospital, the same friend whose mom will become my counselor a year later when I get raped.

Everything about being admitted to hospital felt surreal. It was like I was having an out-of-body experience. The check-in process at the hospital included being asked to show your wrists.

And I remember thinking: "Mmm, nope—things haven't gotten that crazy yet. I'm still just thinking about it, and besides, that's not the way I'll do it..."

I walked into a cold, gloomy ward with four other women who all looked so... sad. No, that wasn't it; they looked frail. The outcasts who couldn't handle the ups and downs of ordinary life. And now I was one of them. I was the youngest person in the room by so many years.

My mom came to visit on that Saturday afternoon. It was so awkward. I felt embarrassed. I could see she didn't really know what to say. I mean, how could she?

The shame and the humiliation, the weight of it all was just so much. And it came to lie heavy and crushing on my chest. Debilitating.

Later in the afternoon, a lady got released to go home.

"So people do leave this place." I think to myself...

But three hours later, that same woman checked back into our ward, sobbing uncontrollably.

"Fuck. So this is what my life's going to look like from now on?"

It's this event that shakes me to my core and brings my mind back to a somewhat normal/sober state.

I'm not even 21 yet—my life has been so easy this far. A loving family, excellent education. Aside from a few music teachers, and the usual high school kids, and boyfriend bs, I've lived the most privileged life.

"Snap out of it, Hanneke! You have big ambitions and visions for life. You want to accomplish amazing and wonderful things. And those things don't include lying in hospital wards and being depressed."

It's right there that I make a commitment to myself.

I will never ever ever end up in a psychiatric ward again. Ever.

And so I got released from hospital a few days later after they had successfully adjusted my medicine, which I vowed to wean myself off of as soon as I was better. The entire experience of medicine that could potentially malfunction at any point and cause havoc whenever it wanted had provoked an intense distrust in me. The very drug designed to bring relief and support, and had so many amazing benefits for others, had left me traumatized.

I didn't want to live a life where the possibility of my antidepressants malfunctioning was always lurking in the shadows. Because my depression was mainly caused by my anxiety, I made a commitment to treat the root of my depression vs. the symptom itself. I was going to create a bright and beautiful future where I learned tools and techniques to manage my anxiety before it could ever anchor down as depression again.

It's that very commitment that gets me through the aftermath of the date rape a year later, which happened to coincide with the very night that I achieved one of my commitments: successfully weaning myself off of anti-depressants without a relapse.

After that night, I had to write my own police statement as the officer assigned to my case was new and inexperienced. Every time they would repeat back what they had in the report, we had to start over because they got all the facts wrong. I was horrified. There were many gynecological exams, and I had to receive HIV-prevention treatment and, of course, counseling.

I told very few people what had happened. I felt so ashamed and stupid. I thought that it was all my fault that this terrible thing happened to me. I had been drinking. I went to his house. If other people knew this, they'd surely judge me.

I was living with my oldest brother in Cape Town at the time. When I told him the story the morning after that terrible night, he didn't judge me at all. Instead, he went into big-brother mode and asked if he could arrange a few people to go and mess up this dude's car. That made me smile. My brother had my back. He was also the one who offered to tell my parents what had happened as I didn't want to hear the disappointment in their voices. I had made all of this out to be my fault.

My dad wanted to talk about it, but I shut them out. I was just too ashamed to share this humiliating event with them.

Someone I could bring myself to confide in was my friend Shirley, who had dropped me at the hospital a year earlier. We were close friends, and her mom was a counselor. She immediately insisted that I see her mom.

When I think back on the counseling I received, I can see how it was my first glimpse into what life coaching was. And it very much helped me to overcome my feelings of self-blame and shame and kept me moving forward. With Shirley's mom's help, I was able to work through the trauma and honor that commitment that I had made to myself in the psychiatric ward.

I decided that I didn't want to press charges. I was about to leave South Africa, and the last thing I wanted was to get caught up in a lengthy legal battle where I'd have to relive the entire horrible thing over and over again. A traumatic event that my brain had automatically blocked from my memory. Why would I want to sit in court while every ugly detail was revealed? Not to mention that I'd have to see my rapist every single day.

When I explained all of this to the new detective who took over my case, we came up with something that would be so much more empowering and help bring closure to the horrible experience.

With his help, I decided to confront my predator in person.

My counselor helped me prepare to face him. She helped me rehearse what I would say. The plan was clear: just stick to the facts.

I remember it being one of those perfect sunny South African days that morning when I went to his house, the same location where the nightmare had taken place. Down a winding road at the foot of Table Mountain with breathtaking views of the City Bowl and Table Bay, it was hard to imagine that something so depraved could occur in such a refined neighborhood. I was extremely nervous but felt safe having the detective by my side. I was armed with the script my counselor and I prepared.

After the detective exchanged a few words with my attacker and showed him my file with all the evidence against him, it was my turn to speak to him. I stood across from him, his kitchen island, creating a safe barrier between us. The words, although simple, came out shaky at first: "You knew I didn't want to do it. You had no right." After delivering my bit, my predator apologized and agreed to pay for all the medical expenses, including counseling.

That younger version of me had so much courage. It was one of the most liberating mornings of my young adult life. And ultimately, it was the action that set me free.

And looking back on all of it now, I so clearly see how this becomes part of the pivotal moment and my first big step into personal growth and self-development, way before it became a fad.

And, of course, it all started with the commitment to myself in the psych ward.

That commitment is what's needed to create change and make dreams happen. No matter the odds and what life may throw at you, there is always a solution, and the way to the solution is the commitment that you make, no matter what: you're never going to stay down. You're going to get up, speak up, and keep going and working towards the life you *do want.*

Facing my rapist diminished the powers of that gnawing thought, the constant internal idea that I couldn't have and be all I wanted to be and have because I wasn't good enough to have it. Now I had a bold example that despite the flaws I thought I had and missteps I believed had gotten me into that dreadful mess, and despite being so hard on myself I was still OK. I could still continue to forge ahead.

This doesn't mean that I don't ever feel "not good enough." Quite the contrary. I feel it often. However, today I understand those thoughts are just that: thoughts, not facts. They are not the truth, and they can't keep me from building and realizing my dreams. They are usually my mind's way of keeping me from stepping into all the realms of my potential and talents. They're a distraction to keep me from following my true bliss.

Our mind plays all sorts of tricks on us, mostly to keep us out of harm's way, of course. But as you can see, my mind's attempt to keep me safe didn't work at all. I still got hurt. Bad things still happened. Everything in your brain was designed and built to help you survive.

And that's what makes your devotion to yourself even more important; without the commitment to do whatever is necessary to attain your deepest desires, you won't get up and face the music. You won't do the hard things. You won't stand up for yourself.

Making this vow will help you to expand into your fullest creative potential. You're here to grow and achieve everything that you're capable of.

And this dedication to become the most exceptional version of yourself will help you grow and build your business beyond what you think is possible. It will keep you focused on what you want, which helps greatly in creating clarity and illuminating the path forward.

Right now, you're channeling that creative force to expand a business that will help you to do what you want when you want to do it. Entrepreneurs are the most amazing manifestors. We literally create something out of nothing. And a big part of this process requires this relentless oath to ourselves and our potential.

Before making this pledge, we have our dreams and visions. We clearly (and sometimes not so clearly) see visions of what's possible, and because we're committed to making it come to reality, we are able to take bold action.

Without this pact to ourselves, those dreams and visions will stay only that. We remain in the dark without it. Only seeing foggy glimpses, always allowing ourselves an out.

We all know people who are in this zone. People who say they're going to do something or say they want to go somewhere, yet you never see them taking steps to achieve that goal. That's because these people haven't made the commitment to themselves. They are still just building castles in the sky, thinking, "wouldn't it be nice?"

And I so get why they stay stuck. Making the resolution that you're going to do whatever it takes for as long as it takes, takes serious courage and bravery. It takes you stepping into the arena to riff on U.S. President Teddy Roosevelt's quote, which Brené Brown cited in her book "Daring Greatly."

"It is not the critic who counts; not the man who points out how the strong man stumbles, or where the doer of deeds could have done them better. The credit belongs to the man who is actually in the arena, whose face is marred by dust and sweat and blood; who strives valiantly; who errs, who comes short again and again, because there is no effort without error and shortcoming; but who does actually strive to do the deeds; who knows great enthusiasms, the great devotions; who spends himself in a worthy cause; who at the best knows, in the end, the triumph of high achievement, and who at the worst, if he fails, at least fails while daring greatly, so that his place shall never be with those cold and timid souls who neither know victory nor defeat."

– THEODORE ROOSEVELT, "THE MAN IN THE ARENA."[2]

You have to strive valiantly too. It takes you being vulnerable, becoming visible. It takes you stepping up, trusting yourself, and leading the way, even if you're not always sure where it's going.

Starting and growing a successful and sustainable business takes guts and tenacity to work and move through your fears; you're not going to let them stop you, no matter what.

You have the power to create the success you're dreaming of. All you need to do is make this pledge to yourself.

A commitment that you're going to do everything possible to align yourself with your goal.

What does this alignment look like? It's an alignment of your thoughts, beliefs, words, and actions to the results you want. When you line all of these up to support your goals directly, you'll achieve the best results possible. I first discovered this concept when reading a book that was based on the Three Principles[3], a philosophy that outlines how our mind, consciousness, and thought work together to create everyone's unique "reality."

Over the years, I've shaped this information, along with my coaching studies, knowledge, and experience, into an equation that has made it easier for my clients to identify where they are out of alignment. They can then make necessary adjustments faster, which of course speeds up the time it takes to achieve their goals.

Throughout this book, I'll explain and dive deeper into this equation, which I've named the Up Level Formula, and equip you with the strategies to identify and make adjustments to uplevel your success as well.

By aligning all the Up Level Formula components, we'll also clearly identify what you stand for, your purpose, and what's important to you. Knowing these core values becomes the cornerstones of your business's foundation, further illuminating the way to your unique success. These values become extremely important when you expand your business and hire more people to work with you. They will directly shape the culture of your business. (I'll explain more on this later in the book too.)

The one thing that almost no one tells you when you're growing your business is just how much this baby is going to push you. How often these values will be tested. How much it's going to require you to stay committed, stay the course, and how much your past life, your demons, your beliefs, and thoughts will be brought back. Haunting and taunting you. And influence your every move.

Denise Duffield Thomas, a money-mindset mentor and author of "Chillpreneur," is often quoted as saying: "New level, old devil." And she's so right.

Our past experiences and stories impact what we think and how we act on a daily basis. And when you're running a business, those demons come into play *a lot!* Especially when you're reaching new levels of success. You may already have noticed how each new level of success brings up weird things like unnecessary or irrational anxiety or fear about the future (or perhaps something totally irrelevant to your business), or stress about money and cash flow, even though you've never had cash-flow issues.

I've been doing continuous self-development work since I was 20, and it still astounds me just how much all those little things that happened when I was a kid or in my young adult life still create havoc in my business right now. If you don't build the awareness of these patterns and behaviors, they'll band together to work against you, and they'll make your road to success way harder than it needs to be.

To create that sustainable and successful business that will allow you the ease and freedom that you crave, you have to do the deep work, we'll tackle in this book.

But all of it starts with you committing that you're going to do the work! If you've already pledged to do whatever it takes to be the most successful version of yourself that you can be, then this work will feel more manageable.

When I made this dedication to myself in that gloomy hospital ward, I had no idea what a profound impact it would have on my life, and later, my business and my clients' businesses. But when I take a microscope to my life to find the determining factor that's allowed me to succeed against all odds: it's my devotion to myself. Even though I still get stuck, the commitment helps me stay the course.

It helped me to get the money together to move to the UK in only three months after that traumatic night I described earlier. It's the same commitment that helped me to manifest my husband on a beach in Portugal, get my Wall Street job, and finally build two award-winning businesses. It's also the commitment that's led me here to serve you.

The commitment is the thing that will drive you to get back up over, and over, and over again.

The commitment inspires you to show up and be a better version of yourself every day.

And when you allow this to sink in, I hope you realize just how much personal power you reclaim when you make a vow like this to yourself.

My commitment to myself and my goal is the instigator that makes dreams happen.

There is always a solution.

When I commit myself to my goal, I expand into my highest creative potential.

When I devote myself to my goals, my business will grow beyond others' limiting opinions.

When I focus on what I want, the path forward immediately becomes clear.

The more committed I am, the more my awareness grows and the easier it is to build a sustainable business.

My commitment inspires me to show up and be a better version of myself every day.

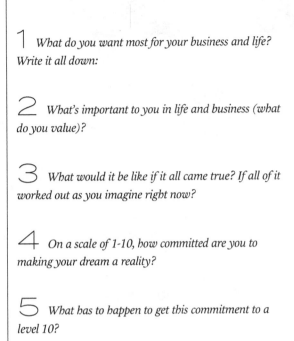

1 What do you want most for your business and life? Write it all down:

2 What's important to you in life and business (what do you value)?

3 What would it be like if it all came true? If all of it worked out as you imagine right now?

4 On a scale of 1-10, how committed are you to making your dream a reality?

5 What has to happen to get this commitment to a level 10?

CHAPTER 2:

Are you suffocating joy?

joy /joi/ Noun:

the emotion of great delight or happiness caused by something exceptionally good or satisfying; keen pleasure; elation.

I lost joy very early on in my life. When I think back on it, I usually only enjoyed the first time I tried something and then my ambition would take over. The force to do better and achieve more felt like the deadly grip of a giant python, slowly squeezing me tighter and tighter.

When I was around 9 or 10, I begged my mom to do ballet. When I tried my first class, I immediately fell in love. A few months later, we had a ballet exam. I remember being excited and having fun during the Cecchetti exam, a rigorous ballet method that pays careful attention to the laws of anatomy. I passed with the highest distinction.

So the next year, a week or so before the exam, I started to pray for that result again. Knowing what I know now about the law of attraction, this was so clearly me focusing and attaching myself to the outcome, trying to control and manipulate it.

I still believe I did really well on that exam, but my report card (and I think almost every report card after that) definitely stated: "The student showed signs of nervousness."

That line pretty much summed up my entire being at the time.

The anxiousness didn't just stop with ballet; it poisoned everything I did. My intensity to achieve and be better and do better grew as I did.

Looking back now, I'm not sure if I was born with all this drive and ambition or whether my surroundings created them.

My parents never put any pressure on me to do better in school. They just always encouraged me to do my best and to have fun with it. ("Fun?!" What does that even mean, I remember thinking.)

Some of my teachers were a different story (remember my music teacher's words to me before that singing performance in Chapter 1).

But teachers aside, I was the one who chose to study classical music and Cecchetti ballet. Although both these practices instilled what it meant to be disciplined and committed, they also came at a cost. They put a certain level of pressure on you as the student. No matter how well you did, it was never—*and could never truly be*—perfect because you were performing the works of great masters.

And thus, it created the ideal scenario to feed the little viper inside me. The story that I wholeheartedly believed was that I wasn't good enough (and I so badly wanted to be!).

Year in and year out, that pressure to be perfect grew bigger and bigger. It became all-consuming, leaving less and less room for fun.

But the harder I tried, the worse I did.

I remember slamming on the keys of the piano, screaming at myself and crying out of frustration of not being able to get a melody right.

In the ballet classroom, my vexation with myself showed all over my face. My teacher misinterpreted my expression as protesting her assertion that I just messed up a dance sequence, so she got even more annoyed with me.

More pressure to do even better. More proof that I wasn't enough. Confirmation that to be accepted, I had to fix or improve something.

The feelings of inadequacy continued to swell, and needless to say, my inner dialogue was a bottomless pit of self-loathing.

In high school, it caused me to be an extremely high-strung kid unpopular with my peers. I would tell them to be quiet. After all, I wouldn't want to get into trouble and get detention or have to wash dishes as punishment in boarding school because my demanding schedule didn't have time for it. Of course, my sternness was misunderstood as being a nerd and a goody two shoes.

I would have epic meltdowns before exams, feeling crushed under the pressure to perform so I could finally stop stressing out and experience the emotions I so desperately wanted to feel: satisfied and calm. I fell for the biggest lie that all of us buy into at one point or another, which is this: One day, when things are perfect, and I'm the best, *then* I'll be able to relax and rejoice in my accomplishments.

Can you relate? How often have you denied yourself a vacation, a spa day, or any other pleasure, stating that someday, once "X" is done, then you'll relax and enjoy yourself? But that day never comes.

A teacher who noticed my puffy eyes after one of those devastating nights once asked me: "Hanneke, what drives you?" My answer: My anxiety.

Of course, in hindsight, my anxiety was just the symptom of all the pressure I was putting on myself. It inflamed my need to fit in, to be liked, to be popular, to be enough just as I was, to love myself deeply and completely.

Most days, this internal strife felt like it was going to suffocate me, spinning my anxiety out of control, resulting in countless sleepless nights that fueled my depression even more.

And my depression swallowed whole whatever successes I was experiencing. The vicious cycle coiled and seeped into my relationships, new jobs, and eventually, my first business. Always leaving me doubtful, burnt out, and raw.

A shadow of my full potential.

An imposter.

Back then, they had a name for people like me: an overachiever. A quick reminder of Wikipedia's definition of that word:

"Overachievers are individuals who 'perform better or achieve more success than expected.' The implicit presumption is that the 'overachiever' is achieving superior results through *excessive* effort."

The meaning of the word further fed the serpent, carrying the shame and worry that we overachievers actually aren't that great. And the only reason we're achieving so-called "success" is because of our tenacity to work harder and longer at things than anyone else. But our achievements can't be trusted because we're defined by a word that clearly states we're doing better than expected.

So then there's no taking our foot off the gas. If we don't work harder, we won't excel. Creating less and less trust in ourselves, creating more and more anxiety for the day when someone will realize that we're a fraud, that we're not that amazing. After all, we're overachievers. This, of course, is what we call imposter syndrome today.

The relentless cycle is always churning, robbing us of joy and excitement for our creations and accomplishments. Like addicts, we're chasing that high, thinking that once we achieve that one big thing, all will be well. And just like with addiction, the high wears off quicker and quicker, and we need bigger goals to satisfy ourselves. It's not a sustainable habit. We grow tired over time, pushed to the edge of burnout. Sometimes pushed over the edge, suffering devastating blows to our health.

Thank goodness the personal-development world has since found a better word to describe us.

High achievers, "someone who is successful in their studies or their work, usually as a result of their efforts."

But then, that shift in perspective doesn't exactly free us of all that internal pressure. As high achievers, our ambition can quickly feel like it's strangling us. When we're in this state, our need to control everything intensifies, further oppressing us.

We have zero faith in ourselves because we're operating from the belief that we're somehow flawed and unworthy. In this frame of mind, we buy into the myth that success takes blood, sweat, and tears. We believe that we have to sacrifice our happiness, our health, and quality time with loved ones. Why? Because success requires suffering. This is where our ego interferes and tells us that it's all in our hands to make things work. *We alone* control everything, and as soon as we loosen our grip, it could fall apart.

And this is the very behavior that will keep your business from growing and scaling successfully.

Your constant worry negates any success you've already accomplished.

Remember when the revenue you make now was your big future goal and how you thought that once you reached this place, you'd stop stressing? Have you stopped stressing yet? Or ever, for that matter?

My guess is no.

By now, there's some other goal you're chasing or things you have to fix, always eclipsing your achievements. You're leaving your soul starved for recognition and exasperating the pressure to work even longer hours.

But how can you work more? I presume that you're already overworked and that this thought keeps you up at night. You may not have any time left to give. You may be feeling exhausted. The joy has been sucked right out of your business.

This is exactly where I was when I burnt down my first business. I had built the Pilates With Hanneke brand up in record time. Three years in, I'd been recognized as one of Boston's top 50 most innovative companies. I was working at six studios across the city, teaching more than 200 students a week, up to eight and nine hours a day, producing and selling DVDs. I saw about 15 private clients a week, many of them famous or high-profile. From the outside, I looked like such a huge success.

The irony was, I wasn't true to my authentic self. The last few years had been a whirlwind of wanting to be better. Competing with others in my industry, playing a lot of defense. Instead of focusing on what my long-term goals were, I felt like I was just playing catch-up, always two steps behind things finally being perfect.

When I think back about how I ran my business, I'm filled with regret. It's crystal clear to me from the beauty of hindsight that I could have built something so much bigger, could have had way more impact if I hadn't deprived myself of fun.

I wish I had taken the time to reflect on what was really possible, but instead, I was mired in my belief that I wasn't good enough, that I had to work harder and longer. I was wrong.

To live up to your fullest potential, you have to stop tangling with the viper weighing you down. You have to step away from your old definition of success and attachment to the idea of being an "overachiever." You have to realize that you, just as you are right now, with or without your business and its success, are enough.

You are complete at this very moment.

Cultivating this awareness will not make you lazy or destroy your ambition. It will, however, help you to work with your aspiration instead of against it. It will allow you to achieve things with less hustle and more ease. (And I promise you that I'll show you how you do this through the Up Level Formula, which we'll cover later in the book.)

At the end of my Pilates career in 2013, I was a shell of what I once dreamt to be. I was so tired. Much like I felt about music and ballet, I resented Pilates. I'd already started my coaching business and brought the same intensity to it. But it very quickly became apparent that what had gotten me to my previous level of success also had snuffed it out. It didn't allow for any bliss.

The hustle wasn't going to give me what I actually wanted. Up until this point, I had lived in the future, in the "one day when then I'll" realm.

But what I really wanted was to be happy NOW!

To have fun NOW!

To experience joy NOW.

And to have all of this in the present, to finally build a sustainable business that was filled with purpose and satisfaction, I had to shed the constricting coil I'd wrapped myself in. I had to incorporate passion and delight now.

And so, with some pep in my step and using the Up Level Formula,

I aligned my business with what I was good at and what inspired me. I stopped obsessing about revenue and competitors and started focusing on the long-term growth of my business instead.

And while traveling the world, taking vacations when and where I wanted, I built another award-winning business. And this time, I had double the fun and half the worry.

And the best part? I got to help so many clients do the same!

Here are the result that one client experienced once they incorporated some of the strategies I share in depth in section two of this book:

> Your guidance has empowered me to achieve an amazing series of slow and steady accomplishments that previously seemed always just out of reach. I want to share with you my pride at this moment, in myself and my business. For the first time in a very long time, I do not feel as if I am a charlatan; what people see on my business's surface now runs very deep. Thanks to our work together, my professional world has grown, matured, stabilized, and literally exudes joy! I am so excited about what's next!
>
> –BRIAN MILAUSKAS, FOUNDER AND OWNER OF KIDSTOCK! CREATIVE THEATER

When I release control, my ambition and
innovation flourish.

I am perfect just as I am.

I am complete.

I am enough.

I achieve success without sacrificing what's
important to me.

I release the myth that success takes blood,
sweat, and tears. I choose ease and flow
instead.

The more I work in alignment with myself and
my values, the more productive I become.

UP LEVEL IT NOW:

1 *How pressure manifests in your body: you might not be aware of the pressure that's pent up inside, particularly frustration and low-grade anxiety. Start to notice what pressure feels like. Write it down:*

2 *Do you often:*

- *Think that success is coupled with high levels of stress, hustling for long hours on end?*
- *Find yourself very attached to how things must play out?*
- *Get fixated on the details and steps of exactly what achieving a goal will look like?*

If you answered yes to any of those questions, it's an indication that you're putting a lot of pressure on yourself.

3 *On a scale from 1 to 10, how pressured do you feel right now?*

4 *How can you alleviate some of that undue pressure or at least drop it down a notch or two?*

5 *What is one thing that you've denied yourself for a very long time? Think of that thing that you always say you'll do/give yourself in the future.*
Example: One day, when I make "X," then I'll take Fridays off. Start taking one Friday a month off right now and then work toward taking every Friday off.

CHAPTER 3:

How to get what you really want

By the time I was in my early 20s and living in London, I was miserable.

I was already on my quest to figure out what I wanted. But it felt hard. I had tried my hand at quite a few things: working in the accounting department of a few companies, being a recruiter. And now I was a Wall Street broker, which is exactly what I thought I wanted.

I still remember being 17, watching the movie "Keeping the Faith" with Ben Stiller, Edward Norton, and Jenna Elfman. She had a big investment job with a corner office in New York City, where she put together massive deals. Watching it back then, I turned to my mom and declared out loud: "One day, I want her job."

And a few years later, I had it. Albeit my offices were in London at the time.

For a little while, I loved that job. I had a corporate credit card and dined at all the exclusive places in London. At age 24, I was earning a salary that translates to well over $175,000 in 2020. [4]

But then I started to notice things that went against my every value and moral: drugs, sexual harassment, and my colleagues' infidelity to their spouses.

All of it was taking a significant toll on my mental health.

I remember one particular day in 2006: we had started drinking with a client at noon and went straight through to 9 p.m. that night. At the end of the night, one client was trying to forcibly kiss me. I kept pushing him away, and he got angry and more aggressive. Thankfully my manager saved me from the tricky situation, suggesting it was time for us to all go home. The next morning I bumped into my manager in the hallway at work, and he casually said: "Miss, I really wanted to fuck you last night."

I believe I was still wasted (something that was totally acceptable in office culture back then), so I laughed it off, thinking it was just a joke. But a few months later, after a team meeting, he asked me to stick around and again expressed that he had "sexual feelings for me."

I started to feel unsafe at work. The men in the office had a saying: When you're a female broker, you're either—and please pardon the crude language—a bike or a dyke. (Yes, that's really what they said, and yes, I'm still appalled.)

It was clear how they thought of me. I was mortified. I remember crying myself to sleep that night, feeling completely trapped. I discussed it with a male colleague, who advised that I shouldn't bring it up to HR because I don't want to be known as "one of those girls."

I just had to sit there and bear it all.

At this point, I'd already figured out that I needed a new job. But what?!

Everything I had tried so far wasn't a fit. What was wrong with me? I couldn't shake that nagging question.

Why couldn't I be like other people who seemed to be happy with any old job? Why couldn't I be more like my colleagues, who seemed just fine showing up drunk, high, or hungover at work and carried on like it was no big deal? Why couldn't I be like those girls who just laughed off all the sexual harassment, seemingly undisturbed by it?

This obsession to find my purpose made me feel like the odd one out. People would often look at me and say, "What's wrong with you?! Why can't you just be content? Most people don't know what they want, and they're fine with it."

All of the input and unsolicited opinions—no matter how well-intended they were—usually made me feel way worse.

Today, of course, I know that this never-ending quest to find your purpose is a telltale sign of someone with an entrepreneurial spirit. I recognize that I would never be happy feeling like I was boxed in by a traditional job.

The constant naysayers who don't share our same drive and big visions make us question and doubt ourselves. And so we grow increasingly restless and exasperated, forcing us to contend with the same question I was asking myself during that time in London.

What is wrong with me?

The inability to uncover what we want makes us entrepreneurs feel like we don't fit in. And it leads to increased frustration with ourselves and the world. It's like a fire raging inside of us, burning up our insides, stealing our joy, and amplifying our anger. It perpetuates that incessant belief that we're not good enough and that we don't belong.

My first boyfriend would lovingly tell me that I was crazy because I was so different from the other girls he knew. My Aquarian spirit was marching to the beat of my own drum, always reaching for what others deemed impossible, daring to be drastically different. And in his eyes that made me cuckoo. For years his words taunted me: Surely I must be crazy to want all this joy, romance, and wealth.

So I started to settle for less than what I really wanted. I tried to tame my expectations. I denied all of my desires. And I pushed them down and down and down. I turned a blind eye to all the crap that was happening at work that made my insides churn. And it was exhausting and making me sick.

Every morning before going to work, I'd gag from all the anxiety and unhappiness. My body revolted against the trauma it would have to face that day. The settling weaved its way into other areas of my life, including my relationships with men.

And so I settled for a relationship with a man who didn't want what I wanted. I remember being in his apartment after he had gone away with a friend for the weekend, excitedly telling him about a perfume I had bought that day and held my wrist for him to smell it. It was Stella McCartney's perfume.

He smiled and said: "Oh, it smells like the stripper from last night."

My heart smashed into a million little pieces. I was crushed. He went upstairs to do something, and I texted a friend about it, who brushed it off as "boys will be boys." No need to leave him.

Looking back, I wish I could give my younger self a big hug and the courage to just walk out without saying goodbye. Because honey, you deserved so much more!

I'd also tell that younger version of myself that she was asking herself the wrong questions.

But unfortunately, there was no older, wiser version of me, and so I stayed. And I overstayed. Because in my mind, I was the crazy one, I was the one who needed fixing, and I was unworthy. I convinced myself that I could mold myself to be the woman he wanted. A woman who'd be OK with him going to strip clubs. Obviously this was just one of those things he should be able to do.

I told myself that not only did I not deserve better, but there was actually nothing better out there. Jaded by the behavior of the men I worked with, I thought that all the respectful men had been wiped out.

My little guardian angel must have heard my future self's advice—or perhaps it was all the prayers my mom was sending me daily. While in London, I definitely put her poor motherly heart through hell as well. I would call her every week in tears. She was thousands of miles away in South Africa, and there was absolutely nothing that she could do for me. Being the devout Christian that she is, she did the only thing she knew to do: she prayed for me daily. And I'm thankful that she did.

The right question finally revealed itself on the skiing slopes of Chamonix, a resort area in France, of all places, where my ski instructor, a very wise man in his 50s, saw deep into my soul.

Every year our company would take clients on a ski trip there. Being from South Africa meant that I had never set foot on a ski hill, let alone worn a pair of skis. So I got my very own private ski instructor for the day. Denis was an Olympic slalom skier.

Needless to say, he was not one bit interested in being on the bunny slopes with a beginner like me making "pizzas" (that's the shape you make with your skis to help you stop, and it's usually the first thing they teach you). But as soon as we met, we instantly hit it off. He was filled with so much joy and zest for life. Being as intuitive as he was, he immediately sensed that I needed a friend. A real friend.

As we talked, Denis not only gave me the right question that I needed to start asking, he also introduced me to a very new term at the time: "life coach." As soon as I returned to London, I hired one!

I owe so much of what followed and what I've accomplished to Denis. He was (and remains) one of the most amazing people I've ever met, and I'm so grateful for his friendship and wisdom.

Back in London, working with my very first coach, Shirley, who also happened to be a South African living in London, I uncovered so much! Through our sessions, we also continued to focus more on the question that Denis first dropped in my head.

What did *I want?*

Up to this point, the focus had very much been what the world wanted from and for me and how I could fit into its confinements. I was fixated on how a boyfriend wanted me to be, what the job wanted me to be, what my family and my friends wanted me to be.

For entrepreneurs, it's essential to forget what everyone else wants you to be. In short: don't do what I did in this chapter.

You are the boss! You are the leader. When we look to others, trying to fit into the limiting (and often disparaging) parameters others have set for us, we lose ourselves, our innovation, and our spirit. These limits rob us of our incredible power to reach our divine potential.

I've had to learn this lesson over and over again. And I've seen so many clients grapple with it too. Empathetic business people usually have great self-awareness. It's a strength that can become a weakness real quick when left unchecked.

And I believe it happens for two reasons:

1. If you're not clear about what you want, it's tough to put your needs first (let alone defend them).

2. If you've been raised to be religious like I was, you probably also grew up with the phrase "turn the other cheek."

I always interpreted this saying to mean that it was wrong to call others out on their bad behavior.

But eventually, my being agreeable and "turning the other cheek" led to getting raped and led to sexual harassment. I spoke out against my rapist, which hopefully stopped him from hurting others. But I often wonder how many more women were hurt because I didn't speak out about the sexual harassment?

Thus getting clear on what you want and making your moral code a priority isn't just necessary to figuring out what you want to be, do, or have. It isn't a self-centered act either; it is, however, a necessary duty to ensure that bad behavior and, in extreme cases, injustices are not perpetuated.

So: What is it that you want?

For such a short question, it's often a difficult one to answer. For one, you've been so focused on those around you that turning the focus on yourself can feel foreign and wrong. Perhaps even selfish.

Once you ask yourself that question, you'll likely struggle with two more: What if I want the wrong thing? What if I get what I want but don't like it?

For me, there were more reasons why I didn't ask myself what I wanted sooner.

My journey to get from South Africa to the UK, and then to the United States, was one of survival. I had a massive student loan to pay off, and failing to get a job and earn decent money meant I'd default on my loan, and that would negatively impact my parents' financial situation. And if I'm honest, I was also running away from that traumatic sexual assault I mentioned earlier.

So for the next few years after university, I ping-ponged from one job to another. I mostly chased the money so I could pay off my student debts as fast as possible.

I remember doing all sorts of crazy things to stretch my money, like living in sketchy houses with strangers for roommates. My thinking was simple: spend as little as possible on accommodations so you can pay off those loans. In London and again in New York, I was tied into a visa that relied on keeping the job I had.

All of the above experiences gave me a very clear understanding of what I didn't want.

I was stuck in a cycle of complaining and focusing on all the things that were happening that I didn't want. My mom, my friends, my boyfriend, and anyone who would listen would know all about what I didn't want. I was so deep in survival mode that there was no bandwidth to clarify what I wanted or what I needed to thrive.

This is often where my clients are when I start working with them. When I ask what they want, the conversation will quickly turn to what is happening in their business that they don't want. This, of course, is our brain's negative bias.

According to Wikipedia: "The negativity bias, also known as the negativity effect, is the notion that even when of equal intensity, things of a more negative nature (e.g., unpleasant thoughts, emotions, or social interactions; harmful/traumatic events) have a greater effect on one's psychological state and processes than neutral or positive things."

In my work with dozens of business owners, we spend a lot of time switching their perspective from this negative bias to the clarity of what they want and what their business needs.

The road to what one wants starts right there in the midst of the not knowing. Because knowing what you don't want informs what you do want.

For example: If you don't want to be overworked or have cash-flow issues anymore, then the opposite of that means: You want to have more time to relax. And you want to make a more significant profit.

If we go deeper and ask: Why do you want to relax more? And why do you want to make more money?—your answer would most likely suggest you believe those two things will give you more freedom to do what you want and when you want to do it.

And when you have this answer, the steps to that goal magically light up for you.

They may not always be easy steps, and they will require you to have the courage to go for it. You'll have to accept the fact that you might fall flat on your face. You'll have to be vulnerable.

And you'll be able to do all of the above because confidence is borne out of clarity.

Knowing what you want will give you the courage and tenacity to achieve what others perceive to be impossible. Clarity will set you free and allow you to stop accepting others' trespasses against you, and help you thrive in the most challenging situations.

I am the leader.

I release the limiting parameters
others set for me.

I choose my divine power and potential.

Knowing what I don't want informs
what I do want.

Clarity sets me free and allows me to thrive.

UP LEVEL IT NOW:

1 *What don't you like about your life and business right now?*

2 *What don't you want for your life?*

3 *What's the opposite of questions 1 and 2?*

CHAPTER 4:

What got you here won't get you where you want to go next

Before learning the art of focusing on what I want versus what I don't want, my mind was all fogged up. It was running in circles from all the catastrophic scenarios that could go wrong. My brain was stuck in a negative bias.

During one of my sessions with my life coach, I remember telling her about this twisted thinking. One part of my brain would argue for all the things that could go right, but then the other would immediately counter it with crazy talk. Like, zombie-apocalypse crazy.

It was then that Shirley gave me one of my very first coaching tools that changed my life. I dubbed it the "what if not?" game. And it goes like this:

Your brain conjures an outrageously pessimistic outcome that could unfold.

Then your mind will contradict these thoughts by reassuring you that such an awful thing won't happen. Your end-of-world thinking will persist and come up with an even scarier proposition: What if my business goes bust?!

And then the fairy godmother side of your brain will argue that that won't happen either. But it's a losing battle because another, more sinister voice will bombard you with worst-case scenarios. Before you can stop it, you're a bundle of frayed nerves, just waiting for Armageddon.

At this point, you're bound to withdraw, isolate yourself from others, and get sucked further into anxiousness. This behavior causes a lot of distraction, sleepless nights, and you don't get anything done.

So how does one stop this vicious cycle?

Simple: You play the "what if not?" game.

Here's how it works:

- As soon as your brain starts with its scary scenario asking, "but what if_____ (fill in your worst nightmare here), you stop it by simply saying: What if not?

- Then your consciousness will try another anxiety-provoking thought, and again you'll meet it with: "What if not?"

- And before you know it, your mind will get bored and will move on to something like, "what's for lunch?"

Go ahead, try it: It's amusing to see how quickly you lose interest and stop the negative-thinking nonsense.

Don't be alarmed if it takes you a little while to get into it. The whole idea here is for you to stop engaging with those negative thoughts. By asking, "what if not?" you're disempowering those ideas.

Later in the book, when I introduce you to the Up Level Formula, we'll do a deeper dive into why it's so important to pay close attention to those thoughts and interrupt them before they cause all the drama.

But for now, stay disciplined and keep at it until your brain wanders off to something more interesting.

After learning this trick, a whole new world opened up for me. My anxiety subsided, and I was able to reflect on the actions that had gotten me to where I was. I had a "boyfriend" who didn't really love or respect me. And I was pursuing a Wall Street career that was going to kill me eventually.

I so clearly remember the morning when I knew that to get what I really wanted out of life, some massive changes would have to be made. All the pushing down and boxing in of what my soul was craving had already turned to rage. And it was slowly getting more and more difficult to control that anger and prevent it from boiling over.

A few days before, a colleague who had been taunting me and spreading rumors that I was sleeping with my boss dropped me in the middle of a deal that we were busy conducting for two clients. Of course, in Barry's douchey little mind, I couldn't just be a hard-working woman with a brain.

When a colleague backs out of a deal, your client usually loses a ton of money. Quick summary (and very basic explanation) of how a foreign-exchange deal works: On the back end of your client saying they want to buy or sell US dollars for Euros at a specific quoted price, they're also locking in an ideal exchange rate for the swap of USD to EU. That deal happens on a different desk called the spot desk, and that exchange rate is updated every second.

So listening to spot brokers is like listening to those seagulls in "Finding Nemo" going: "Mine, mine, mine, mine…," but instead of the word "mine," these guys are quoting numbers. Needless to say, with spot prices updating every second, if your colleague drops you on a deal where everything was supposed to line up with that exact exchange rate, your client is going to be extremely annoyed. And they may even decide to never deal with you again, which means you'll lose future commissions.

It's a stressful situation to find yourself in. And what that meant for me at that very moment was this: I completely lost my cool.

That's right: On a floor of 800 mostly men, with only four female brokers at the time, this South African went batshit crazy. My rage poured out of me; I was like a mad person. I screamed and cussed and was about to lunge across the desk's monitors to get to Barry and punch his lights out. No, actually, I wanted to strangle him at that very moment! All the while, Barry kept screaming back, telling me I was crazy and a silly bitch. It was chaos. It goes without saying that our quarrel got the attention of the entire floor. My boss and the other colleagues on our desk were frantically trying to calm us down but to no avail. Eventually, I was ordered to step outside to cool off.

I wasn't a smoker, but that day I wished I were. I needed something, anything to take the edge off. I called my brother, who was also living in London, to process what had just happened, and as I paced downstairs outside the office, I knew I had hit my breaking point.

I saw a future vision of myself at age 40: Resentful, bitter, and angry for never listening to my inner calling that had tugged at me for years to pursue a career that would bring me fulfillment. I'd probably have liver cancer from all the stress and years of binge drinking and little sleep. I'd have a slew of ex-husbands, paying alimony for multiple kids I never saw. I would have accrued such a high cost of living over the years, which would limit my options to do anything else. I'd be what the industry called golden handcuffed to this job that I hated.

At age 24, that was *not* the future I wanted.

I was done. I had hit rock bottom.

Remember the implementation question I posed in Chapter 2 that helps you to pinpoint where you are with a feeling on a scale from 1 to 10?

Well, if you had posed that question to me that day—how angry did I feel on a scale of 1 to 10?—I'd be at a 100 (and no, that's not a typo). I'd break the fucking scale.

I finally saw that this work environment and my toxic relationship were bringing out the very worst parts of me.

The only way I knew to survive in this hostile habitat (and to be taken seriously) was to become more aggressive, shielding myself in a blanket of constant hate and fury or by numbing it all by drinking too much.

This bitter, angry woman I was slowly becoming wasn't who I wanted to be. I didn't want the life that I saw at 40 if I continued following this career trajectory.

When I was 16, I got this adorable Valentine's card that read: "Always stay the bubbly sparkly person that you are!"

The bubbles had gone flat. Getting to where I now found myself, I had pushed to the curb all the aspects of my personality that I (and others) enjoyed. The only way back to that kind and loving person was to choose a new way of being. And to do that, I'd have to start doing things differently. I'd have to make different choices.

You can't find peace when you're constantly showing up prepared to fight.

Back then, it appeared that I had it all. I scraped up the money to move to London in just three months. I overcame depression. And while I was overcoming my battle with depression, I was raped and survived the trauma of that, too.

Once I was in London, I landed a prestigious job in what was then the financial capital of the world.

So yes, from the outside, you might have said, "But you made it!"

Not quite. Instead, I felt like I was at war every day. I wasn't happy. The excitement and perk of a company credit card and glamour of the job had lost their appeal. Society's definition of success, the idea that you do whatever it takes to make it big (no matter your morals), just wasn't for me.

I realized that all my actions up to that point sprang from fear—tainted with that growing rage that I had just unleashed all over the brokerage floor. The harder I pushed to get through, the harder it all got. And it was all so exhausting. I was exhausted.

What got me here was a terrified girl who felt so trapped, someone who was gagging every morning, who wasn't sleeping, and who was a nervous wreck.

While working with my entrepreneurial clients, I've discovered the same pattern in them as well.

When we first start our businesses, we run on the thrill and excitement of it all. The promise of big shiny success. We do *everything* we can to grow our companies, and we do most of it all by ourselves. Then the prestige wears off, and we go into survival mode; we start to worry and obsess over our business like it's the only thing that matters. We push and hustle hard and work nonstop. And in the process, we start turning a blind eye to who we really are and what we truly value. There is no room for fun, and we deny ourselves any rewards, pushing them to another day that never comes.

And then we reach a point where we're no longer experiencing the passion and joy that once propelled our ambition. We hit a plateau, a painful place where we're still spinning our wheels like crazy but see very little or no progress.

You start to feel how exhausted you are, and, just like me, your exhaustion can and will turn into the rage and frustration I felt when I almost strangled my colleague. And just like that, a fucked-up relationship with your business is created where it pulls out all of your worst personality traits.

You've reached your breaking point. And it's here where the people closest to you bear the brunt of it all.

You feel guilty. You're overwhelmed and don't know how to change things to create the blissful freedom you once dreamt of. And worst of all, you are starting to lose hope that there is a way for you to be as successful as you want to be without giving up every ounce of yourself and your happiness.

You're sucked dry, and there's nothing left to give. At this point, it's crucial to understand that the results you dream of won't come from your current actions.

You hold the power. And you can choose to design your life and your business to be what you want them to be. To achieve this, you'll have to act in ways that are aligned with what you want. And it's going to feel uncomfortable at first because you'll be taking steps in new directions that will feel unfamiliar, maybe even terrifying.

But I promise you that it will be worth it. And I'll be there with you every step of the way. In the rest of this book, I will guide you and show you what actions you need to take to arrive at the outcome you desire. Together we're going to create the freedom and ease you crave. I'm going to help you transform into a confident business owner who works less and experiences more fun.

And when you allow yourself to stay in the room, to do the exercises I give, to keep reading, to stay committed, and to believe in yourself, you, my dear, are going to experience so much more joy and abundance than you ever thought possible.

The most beautiful thing of all is that once you choose to go on this journey with me, you will no longer feel like you're on the battleground every day. Things will start to become easier. Sometimes it will feel like things just fall into place for you.

A short while after that rage-filled day when I committed to start doing things differently, I finally mustered up the courage to break up with the man who was causing me so much heartache. I immediately said a little prayer, asking the universe to please move him back to Germany. I knew that if he stayed in London, I wouldn't be strong enough to stay away from him.

A few weeks later, he was transferred back to Frankfurt. (And although it wasn't a clean break, the distance between us helped me to finally get over him.)

Boom! The first proof that when I showed up and took different actions, life seamlessly worked itself out in my favor.

One of my clients who runs an in-home-chef service company would always say that when she started her business, she was in the kitchen chopping the onions because that was what was required of her at the time. As her business grew, she kept thinking that she had to stay in the kitchen. But doing the grinding and hustling in the kitchen meant that she wasn't taking action as the owner and CEO of her business. Staying in the kitchen and chopping those onions meant that she got increasingly frustrated. She was overworking to keep her business running, and it was nearly impossible to expand.

When we started working together, I helped her to see how these actions weren't leading her to what she wanted. Together we helped her to stop chopping the onions and firmly and confidently assume her position as the visionary of her business. By showing up and doing the tasks of a founder, she grew her business, even in the face of a pandemic.

For me, doing things differently happened incrementally, but I remained focused. And a year or so after that quarrel with my colleague, I persuaded my boss to transfer me to our offices in New York City.

I had met a lovely man on a beach in Portugal who was the complete opposite of everyone I had ever dated (more on this serendipitous story in Chapter 20!). He lived in Boston, and so working in New York would shorten our long-distance romance.

A year later, in 2009, despite continuing traumatizing events at work, it all finally came together, and I broke up with the dysfunctional career that was making me miserable.

I did all of the above by following the steps I've told you about so far:

1. I stayed true to the commitment I made to myself seven years earlier while hospitalized with depression, to create a future where I was happy (Chapter 1). I showed up every day with that intention in mind.

2. I learned to release some of the pressure I put on myself for things to be perfect (Chapter 2). This continues to be a work in progress. By allowing myself and things to be imperfect, I've gotten way more satisfaction out of life than ever before.

2. I figured out what I wanted by following the crumbs of what I didn't want (Chapter 3). Those crumbs led me to the most fulfilling life that I would never have been able to dream up for myself.

3. And I learned that creating an abundant and happy life, filled with all the things I wanted, required me to do things differently (Chapter 4). I moved to Boston to be with the man who brought out the very best in me and to pursue a career as a Pilates instructor, which gave me more freedom and flexibility to visit my family in South Africa.

I want you to remember that the journey to fulfillment isn't a linear path. Creating both a business and life that brings you satisfaction comes by setting an intention to do so and taking messy action toward it. It's those tiny little incremental changes that we implement daily that eventually add up and create a massive avalanche of sustainable happiness and success.

When I show up and take different actions,
life seamlessly works itself out in my favor.

When I act in alignment with my values,
I create success with ease.

The more fun I have, the faster
my business grows.

I hold infinite power.

I choose to design my life and business
to be what I want them to be.

It's normal to feel uncomfortable when I'm
taking steps in new directions.

I give myself permission to allow my actions to
be messy, and I trust that it will all work out.

The more I act in alignment with what I want
the easier it becomes to achieve success.

1   *What have you accomplished so far?*

2   *What are the actions that got you to those accomplishments?*

3   *What felt hard?*

4   *What actions will make the journey more fun?*

Cultivating Awareness for Growth

CHAPTER 5:

Becoming friends with fear

While working with a client and helping her to expand her business to multiple locations, we kept bumping up against the F-word.

Her fear.

I do a lot of work with clients around this feeling, and it's not just because most of us despise feeling anxious. According to research: "abnormal levels of fear and anxiety can lead to significant distress and dysfunction and limit a person's ability for success and joy of life."[5]

And as you know, I'm all about helping business owners achieve success with less stress and all the joy. Because I've experienced boatloads of fear in my life, one of my deepest regrets is how I allowed my anxiety to suppress joy. Fear robbed me of the excitement of performing. Who knows what could have happened to my singing career if I had learned sooner what I'm about to teach you in this chapter? Could I have been the next Taylor Swift? Probably not. But it's fun to dream and imagine what might have been.

When we allow fear to rule us, we become tiny unsatisfied versions of who we really are. We allow our amazing talents to fade, never developing them to become superpowers that bring us fulfillment and success. I think we can all agree that that's the last thing any of us want. We are here to step into the most glorious dimensions of our authentic selves.

And that's exactly where my client found herself during one of our sessions. Frustrated with the knowledge that her fear was blocking her full potential, she asked:

"So when am I going to stop feeling all this fear?"

Being the no-BS business coach that I am, I gave her the honest answer: Never.

I know what you might be thinking. "WTF, that's it? I'm out. Next book, please."

Stick with me here because I'm about to transform your whole perception of the nasty F-word.

We've been conditioned our whole lives to see fear as a bad thing. Since we were little kids, our parents would say something like, "Oh, don't worry, honey." Or, "You don't have to be scared." And one of my not-so-personal favorites: "Don't feel anxious."

Thanks. Thanks a lot.

Of course, these words were shared out of love and to comfort us, but, unfortunately, they instilled the notion that fear should be... well, feared. So from then on, whenever we had to self-soothe, we'd say to ourselves: "Stop worrying."

But you didn't. Instead, your body sent you signals that things weren't OK: your hands went clammy, your heart pounded faster and louder, and made you wanna puke. This experience, while visceral, is not fun.

That's why you so badly wished it would go away. But it wouldn't subside. It seemed to always be lingering in the shadows, ready to pounce and debilitate any expansive action you tried to take.

And so, for all your life, you've been at war with fear. And you've been losing that battle.

I used to be in that same fight. I've suffered from anxiety attacks since I was 16, and I still occasionally get them. And just like you, I used to absolutely fucking hate feeling nervous. I'd curse its very existence. And as I did, the feeling swelled up and consumed even more physical space.

Fear followed me everywhere. It was there during every ballet exam and singing performance. It was present the day I went to face my rapist. It was there when I moved to London when I asked for a transfer to New York City. And it was especially felt every time I created something new in my business.

In short, fear always presented itself when I was advancing to the next stage of my natural evolution. The personal-development world refers to this as stepping outside your comfort zone. I like to think of it as you stepping into your next level of growth and expansion.

You might have even seen this (very overused) graphic:

The image implies that the open space outside these two circles is filled with stormy waters and unfamiliar territory.

This reminds me of a quote by American author Elizabeth Gilbert in her book "Big Magic":

"Fear is always triggered by creativity because creativity asks you to enter into realms of uncertain outcome. And fear hates uncertain outcomes. This is nothing to be ashamed of. It is, however, something to be dealt with." [6]

Your business will dictate that you develop and elevate your game often. Failure to do this will result in your business stagnating. It will also make the process of expansion excruciating for you—the total opposite of what you want the experience to be. You're reading this book to have more fun on the journey to prosperity.

I would often hear people say: you just have to take action despite fear. And I did. And like I said, it made me wanna puke. There had to be an easier way, and I was going to find it.

To do so, I had to know why I was feeling fear in the first place. Why *did* anxiety spike in the face of unknown outcomes? What was fear's purpose?

I suspect you already know the answer: The emotional response of fear is activated to keep you safe. Being from South Africa, a country with the third-highest crime rate in the world[7], I used to hear the word "safety" and think about it only in terms of physical safety. That drove me bonkers, but what I wasn't able to grasp back then was the reality that fear is also about your emotional well-being.

How was I supposed to coexist with such an unruly and irrational emotion?

As noted in a Smithsonian magazine story about how the brain processes fear: "It is a fundamental, deeply wired reaction, evolved over the history of biology, to protect organisms against perceived threat to their integrity or existence."[8]

Finally, I understood why I felt a paralyzing amount of fear while working on Wall Street. It also explained why it was so difficult and nerve-wracking for me to market my business and make it more visible. It went against my moral standards.

Above and beyond physical danger, fear is triggered whenever we attempt to:

1. Do something that we were taught was wrong.

2. Go against a specific perceived cultural or family code.

3. Try anything that experience has taught us leads to undesired results.

Or, more simply put: Fear will always be with us. There's no getting rid of it. Instead of viewing anxious feelings as something we should exterminate, we have to learn how to live with them harmoniously.

It was time to put down my weapons of destruction and stop treating fear as the enemy.

Around that time, a friend shared some advice that helped me reframe how I viewed fear. It was a quote from actor Josh Pais' online course "Committed Impulse," where he helps actors and entrepreneurs get over limitations imposed by their body and mind. (You might remember Josh as the assistant medical examiner Borak on the TV show "Law & Order," or perhaps one of the eight different characters he played in various "Law & Order" spin-offs.)

Here's what Josh said:

"Be nervous. Be very nervous. And be nervous now. If there is nervousness in you in this moment, or in any moment for that matter, feel it. Nervousness is a little creature in you that just wants to run around. Might as well let the

little creature run through the field and do its thing. It will be napping under a tree before you know it. If, however, you try to trap that little creature and squash it in a cage, it will kick and chew on the bars and get covered in its own stinky." [9]

Here are the three ways this quote helped me:

1. By accepting my fear, I was able to feel the feeling with less judgment.

2. Viewing nervousness as a "little creature" instead of a giant scary monster allowed me to be less afraid of it. Up until that point, I had a fear of fear, which meant that I would constantly be dreading the next time that I'd get nervous again. This translated into feelings of low-level anxiety at all times, which made me hate fear even more.

3. It also showed me why the "what if not?" game I taught you in Chapter 4 worked so well. When we allow ourselves to feel fear without engaging it, it passes through us faster and wreaks less havoc.

Reframing my perception of fear helped me to make it my loyal companion. As a result, I could fall right back asleep when I did wake up in an anxious sweat at night. And I wasn't the only one. Another client had this to say after I helped him befriend his fear: "I haven't slept this well in a long, long time. I'm really excited about it."

It also sped up my progress. When I was setting goals and taking action, I no longer looked for the route that was going to cause me the least amount of anxiety. Instead, I got curious about my nervous feelings. I'd ask myself: Why am I feeling so anxious right now?

And, just like when you're talking to a friend, I'd keep drilling down until I uncovered the root of the fear and the worst-case scenario, which was usually the fear of failing.

Failure, of course, has many faces. Once I identified exactly what form of it I was most afraid of, I'd ask: So if that happened, what would you do then?

Shifting my perception from animosity to a healthy interest in fear helped me develop a contingency plan. And that plan made me feel safe, physically and emotionally. With my bases covered, it freed me to come up with more innovative ideas and creative solutions, and I could take bolder actions with more ease. I gained so much clarity. I finally stopped worrying so much and moved forward faster.

Which brings us to the client I mentioned at the beginning of this chapter, who asked when she would stop feeling all the fear. Once I helped her to adopt this process, her business vision became clear. In less than two years, she was able to grow her business from one to three locations.

Here's how she is dealing with fear now:

> I try to figure out if my fear is coming from something valid (maybe I'm taking too risky of a business move) or, more likely if it's coming from self-doubt. I reassure myself that I'm safe, and at the end of the day, I know I will likely have to 'feel the fear and do it anyway,' as they say. I remind myself that facing my anxiety is good for me emotionally and occupationally, even if it feels bad. I also reflect on the other times I took action despite my fear. Usually, this reflection helps me see that it either worked out great or that I now no longer experience fear about that specific action.
> – COURTNEY CULNANE, FOUNDER AND CEO OF LEEWARD COUNSELING

Fear makes us stronger and more effective if we allow it to do so. So stop trying to kill fear off. Accept it and let it be the very engine that informs what action you should take next.

This blueprint is another crucial step on the path to helping you create a business that brings you all the satisfaction you're craving. Now grab your fear, give it a big hug, and let's dive into the process that will exponentially upgrade your results.

It's normal for me to feel fear.

Fear helps me learn, grow, and improve.

Acknowledging my fear helps it dissipate.

It's OK to feel fear and do it anyway!

When I allow myself to feel and accept my
fear, it makes me stronger and more effective.

1 *What are you afraid of?*

2 *Why is that freaking you out?*

3 *What is the worst-case scenario that you fear could happen?*

4 *What will you do when the worst-case scenario plays out? (When you run through catastrophic scenarios and come up with a plan that you can implement, you can then stop worrying because you've got it covered. You know what you'll do when it all goes to hell in a handbag, which it probably won't.)*

5 *Now that you have a contingency plan, give your fear a big hug and say: I accept you and thank you for being my informant! And if it's being stubborn, don't forget to play the "what if not?" game with it. What if it all works out in your favor?*

CHAPTER 6:

If only they had told us sooner

*"Happiness is when what you think, what you say,
and what you do are in harmony."*

– MAHATMA GANDHI

While working with my life coach, she recommended a book that was a complete game (and life) changer.

In his book "Somebody Should Have Told Us! (Simple Truths for Living Well)," Jack Pransky dissected the idea that not everything we think is true.[10]

That fascinated me. He explained that our brain's habit of treating every thought as if it's set in stone is a huge reason why we experience so much unhappiness, anxiety, and even depression. Reading "Somebody Should Have Told Us!" drastically altered my thinking and changed my life.

Pransky's book was my first insight into how the brain works. I became somewhat obsessed and since have done a lot of reading and research on how our thoughts become things. Now you may be sitting there going, "Huh? Can you please be more specific?" Stick with me, and in this chapter, I'll show you exactly what I mean.

But first, let's take a look at this diagram on the right. Here's a quick breakdown of what's happening:

Situation:
You're going about your day, and something happens to you (it happens outside your body). And before you have a thought or a feeling about it, the situation gets filtered through a lens.

Lens:
This is the filter through which you see the world. Think of it as sunglasses with lenses that are tinted in a unique and specific shade. Your culture, how you were parented, your social status, your relationships

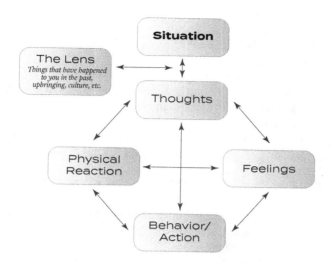

with other people, and everything else that's ever happened to you since you were born, plus the thoughts you think over and over again—these all have an impact on the shade or tint of your glasses. They inform how you will see the world. You've created a little lens, representing your deep-rooted beliefs about life and your abilities, what's possible and what's not. This filter dictates what to expect, based on what's happened in the past, which then results in you having specific thoughts about it.

Thoughts:
Through that lens, the thoughts that your brain will start to produce will either be positive, negative, or neutral.

Feelings:
If that thought was negative, you will have a negative feeling about it. If the thought was positive, you'll experience a positive feeling.

Behavior / Action:
Based on the type of thought you have (negative, neutral, or positive), you'll take some sort of action.

Physical Reaction:
Study.com defines it as follows: "A physical reaction occurs when molecules undergo a molecular rearrangement to produce a physical change.

The molecules are not chemically altered. As a reminder, molecules are two or more atoms linked by chemical bonds."[11]

This means the physical reaction is where and how you'll process that feeling in your body, which will continue to give your brain and body feedback. And then more thoughts and feelings will be brought about, creating a constant feedback loop.

As I mentioned in Chapter 1, I've configured all of the above into a simple equation and dubbed it the Up Level Formula:

Beliefs + Thoughts + Language + Feelings + Actions = **Results**

Note that I added language in this equation since that's a direct insight into your thoughts. And the lens has been replaced with beliefs.

Let's consider an example.

As I've mentioned before: growing up in a conservative culture like South Africa's, I experienced many instances of "don't do that, because what are the neighbors going to think?" and "be humble at all cost."

That led me to believe that one must always try to blend in, never be too this or too that, and whatever you do, don't toot your own horn.

Being conditioned to think like that became the lens through which I viewed the world.

As a result, I believed it was wrong to be too visible and or talk about my accomplishments unless I was asked about them. If I did, I risked being viewed as not humble, and I'd embarrass myself. And what would others think of me then?!

Now, let's fast forward a few decades, and I'm starting my own business, which required lots of marketing and visibility and telling people why they should work with me.

Viewing my options through the lens of limitations—"be humble, don't rock the boat, and fit in at all costs"—gave me the following thoughts:

"What you're doing is totally wrong!"

"People are going to think you're being boastful."

Those thoughts resulted in these feelings:

- Anxiety. (It felt unsafe to put myself out there.)

- Fear. (Of what others would think of me, which would lead to being rejected and ending up alone.)

- Anger. (I wanted to succeed but wasn't allowed to do what it took.)

- Frustration. (For feeling all of the above.)

And all those thoughts and feelings manifested in my body: My chest felt tight, my tummy was turning and twisting in knots. I had headaches, anxiety attacks, and problems sleeping.

It also bled into my language, constantly saying things like: "Yeah, I can't do that because ___ ." Fill in any excuse under the sun. Or "In South Africa, we don't do that."

It's clear that the ingredients of my Up Level Formula were misaligned, which influenced the actions I was taking. I was procrastinating, not marketing as boldly as I could, not doing good business planning, etc. Which obviously had an impact on my results.

In short: My thoughts were becoming things that I didn't desire.

So how does one rectify this? How do you get the results you want?

Simple: make little upgrades to every part of the Up Level Formula. Becoming aware of where things are out of whack in the formula will help you to deconstruct and then reconstruct your old conditioning to achieve your objectives.

Let's take a closer look at how those thoughts become beliefs.

Beliefs + **Thoughts** + Language + Feelings + Actions = Results

---

I think we can all agree that:

1. We do have a lot of thoughts every day. Some research even suggests that humans have between 12,000 and 60,000 thoughts per day.[12]

2. And when we look at the extremely divided world we live in, it's also clear that one doesn't easily change someone else's mind on something they already deeply believe in. The same logic applies to our own ingrained thoughts: Once we've established a certain way of thinking, it's hard for us to change that narrative.

But I don't like assumptions, so let's zoom in a little deeper into our magnificent grey matter to see what the science tells us about how thought patterns work.

Brain cells are constantly communicating with one another. The more these brain cells communicate, the stronger the connection between them becomes. Psychologist Deann Ware states that "these messages that travel the same pathway in the brain over and over begin to transmit faster and faster." And over time, those repetitions will become automatic.[13]

In my anatomy training to become a Pilates instructor, we were told that it takes approximately 10,000 repetitions for a new neural pathway to be etched into the brain.

Wikipedia defines a neural pathway as "the connection formed by axons that project from neurons to make synapses onto neurons in another location, to enable a signal to be sent from one region of the nervous system to another."

Now that we understand the brain and its functioning even better, we know this:

1. You think so many of the same thoughts because your brain has been programmed to think in a specific way.

2. If you don't like what you're thinking, it is possible for you to change those patterns by laying down new neural pathways.

Let's say your thinking is mostly negative. You can think of these pessimistic neural pathways as a massive highway that's been built over time. By now, the thought just hops on that highway, and wee, it's barreling toward its destination: Negative Nancy-ville.

To reach a state of optimism, we have to start building a new road. And it will be a small road at first. Your job is to continue to keep the thought on the small and narrow until it becomes that big massive highway and the old one will fade in the rearview mirror.

And the very first step to starting construction on the new optimistic neural pathway is accepting that not everything you think is the truth.

Next, you'll have to divert traffic to the new road. We do this with something called pattern interrupters. These are exercises that will disrupt the thoughts that are causing worry and negativity.

Some of them may sound a little "out there," but remember that commitment you made in Chapter 1, my friend. So far in this chapter, I've given you all the scientific evidence showing how the brain works. And now it's time to start putting that research and the Up Level Formula into action to rewire your brain to achieve the success you deserve.

I'll share multiple exercises. Try all of them once or twice, and then decide which ones you like and move forward with those.

Here are some interrupters that can help you:

1. The "what if not?" game:
The very first exercise that helped me was the one I shared in Chapter 4: The "what if not?" game.

A quick recap on how it works: when you have a catastrophic thought, instead of engaging with it, simply say: "What if not?" When your mind follows it with another disaster that may unfold, repeat the question: "what if not?" And continue until your brain gets bored—trust me, it won't take long.

Using this tool to interrupt catastrophic thinking as soon as you become aware of it is huge to change your brain's behavior.

2. Tapping of Emotional Freedom Technique (EFT):
The Tapping Solution gives a great explanation of what tapping is: "Like acupuncture and acupressure, Tapping is a set of techniques that utilize the body's energy meridian points. You can stimulate these meridian points by tapping on them with your fingertips – literally tapping into your body's own energy and healing power."[14]

You can watch a bonus video I prepared on tapping by visiting our book resources page at hannekeantonelli.com/book-bonus.

I love tapping because it reinforces self-love. And most of the time, our negative thinking is a reflection of our negative self-talk. For instance: when I compare myself to others, I get jealous. When I'm jealous, I'm super judgmental about myself. All of a sudden, nothing that I've accomplished or done is good enough.

Someone who loves themself doesn't think this way.

And that's why I love EFT. It acknowledges your thoughts and feelings, which is essential to get back on track with thinking positive thoughts. And then it reinforces unconditional self-love by ending with: "I deeply and completely love and accept myself."

So no matter what, you love yourself.

3. Wearing an elastic band around your wrist:
I first learned this trick from author Denise Duffield-Thomas ("Chillpreneur"), who's been my money mindset mentor for years.

How it works:

This exercise is specifically intended for those tough repetitive negative thoughts that you keep having about yourself: "I'm not good enough," "I'm never going to be able to do or accomplish X."

You put a hair elastic or any other elastic band around your wrist. Every time you catch yourself thinking something you don't want to think, you pull the elastic back and let it snap against your skin. This does go against what you might have been taught in therapy and even a little contradicting to tapping as well. Remember that in coaching, we do often take a more tough-love approach.

Please note: This exercise is not intended to promote self-harm. This exercise is ONLY to be done with a small little band around your wrist.

Snapping the elastic band will give a very tiny sharp pinch on your wrist, which will send a message to your brain saying: "Hey, when I think those negative thoughts, I feel a little sting, and I don't like it." And this association will deter your brain from having that thought.

In essence, it works similar to when you were little, and your mom gave you a little spank at the same moment as you were doing something wrong or when training a dog with a shock collar. (Granted, I realize both of these methods might be controversial to some readers. So try this next step instead.)

4. Using the "We don't think that thought anymore" statement:

This one is great, especially if you don't like the idea of the elastic band. When you catch yourself thinking a thought that is out of alignment with what you want to achieve, you simply say: "No, we don't think that thought anymore."

Not all my thoughts are true.

I get to choose what thoughts
I attach weight too.

I get to choose what I think.

I align my thoughts, words, and actions
to attain the results I want.

UP LEVEL IT NOW:

1 *Pick one of the pattern interrupters from this chapter to disrupt any thinking pattern that's no longer in alignment with what you want to achieve.*

2 *Choose your favorite mantra above and repeat it as often as possible—notice what happens.*

3 *Listen to my interview with Jack Pransky for an in-depth understanding of the Three Principles, the philosophy that played an integral part in laying the foundation for my Up Level Formula. To hear how it has helped people overcome adversity, visit hannekeantonelli. com/book-bonus*

CHAPTER 7

The beliefs that determine your success

A s I mentioned in the previous chapter, beliefs are simply thoughts that we think over and over again, and along with our experiences, they shape and color the way we see the world. When I was in high school, I loved math and did pretty well at it, scoring a solid "B" on higher-grade tests. I wasn't viewed as gifted or anything. I just loved using that part of my brain that needed to figure something out versus memorizing a whole list of dates, like you had to do in history or biology.

Being a little nerd, I also had a deep-rooted belief that I wasn't actually that smart; the only reason I was doing well at school was because I was studying my butt off. This belief came from another teacher's words to me a few years earlier. He pulled me aside and said that I must be careful of working so hard and doing too well, as it was not sustainable.

Looking back, I think the point he was trying to get across was for me to also have some fun and not put so much pressure on myself. However, my 15-year old self didn't interpret his message the way he intended. Instead, I took it as proof that he knew I wasn't that smart and overachieving.

Fast forward a few years, and it was time to make career decisions, and like most people, I was a little lost on what to pursue. Deep down, I wanted to become a ballet dancer, but my parents advised that this was a pipe dream and that getting a degree in that would be risky business, especially living in a place like South Africa where the economy wasn't doing that well.

Naturally, those were their beliefs, based on what they had experienced over the years and then passed down to me, too.

So I showed up at the guidance counselor's office believing the misconceptions that "I'm not that smart; I just work hard" and "the economy is too bad to follow your passion."

To my great surprise, I scored 100% on her math test and was the first person in 16 years to achieve that. Based on that and the other tests she had me do, she suggested that I pick a career in actuarial science. Becoming an actuary would mean that I would use statistics and my love of numbers to predict uncertain future times and mitigate risk. I remember my dad spilling a proud tear. He was a numbers guy too, and his little girl was going to follow in his footsteps.

When it was just me and the counselor in the room again, I protested that this must be a fluke because, look: I usually scored a "B" in math classes, and I couldn't possibly have a high-pressure job like that because I suffer from depression!

The counselor then gave me advice that would stick with me for life. In fact, it's something that I tell my clients often too.

She said: You can't rely on what you view as limitations as your crutch. If you want to reach your full potential, you have to put them down.

That blew my mind. It would take another few years before I could fully grasp her advice and throw away the crutches.

I left the counselor's office super excited. I was going to become something super cool: an actuary—and my dad was so freaking proud of me!

I started making some phone calls to ask other people who were in the field what it was like and if they thought I could do it. (Helpful hint: That's a terrible idea.)

When we ask others for their opinions, they give us advice through their personal lens. Just like your lens, theirs have been tainted by experience and perception too. And when it comes to other people, we usually have a set expectation of what we think they are capable of as well. This is why it's so hard for you to make a decision when asking other people for their two cents.

In coaching, we call that their agenda. Typically, coaches won't work with friends because the lines are blurred, and the coach can't be 100% objective.

We view everyone in our lives a certain way, and we box them into that specific thing. That stems from the idea that people never change—which, by now, we've proved isn't true. People can change. It does take work, but it is totally possible.

The reason why people don't often change is that the process of change requires both internal execution and external support.

Back then, I didn't have faith in my intellectual abilities (internal), and thus, I went to friends (external) to validate that I'd be successful in that specific career. As a result, I got more and more confused and had less and less trust that I'd succeed as an actuary.

So even though I got accepted into the university's actuarial science program, my doubts and other people's opinions made me change my major the first day of enrollment.

If we analyzed my two limiting thoughts—that I wasn't actually that intelligent and that because of my depression, I wouldn't be able to handle a high-pressure job—we'd see that both of them translated to: I'm not good enough.

I'm sure you can come up with a bunch of similar scenarios from your past that shaped what you think you can accomplish. And if we zoomed in, they'd break down to one of the following:

I'm not enough.
I'm not worthy.
It's not safe.
I'll end up alone.

We have many different limiting beliefs, and my clients have often mentioned the ones I just listed.

And when you challenge those beliefs, you'll suddenly remember previous scenarios where these doubts played out. The more we perpetuate these restrictive narratives, the more we strengthen and validate them. It's a vicious cycle that keeps us stuck and unable to reach our full potential.

This happens because of something called confirmation bias: "the tendency to interpret new evidence as confirmation of one's existing beliefs or theories."

This means that your brain is always looking for evidence that what you believe is correct and true. The problem is that when your brain does this, it ignores other data.

Here's a real-life example: Remember when you got your new car?
Out of nowhere, you started spotting it all over the road.

But why? Did they suddenly make and sell more of these models? Nope. They were always there. Your attention has just shifted to them because of your awareness of your new car.

What we focus on expands.

Our beliefs act like a giant magnifying glass, forever amplifying situations that support them.

Why is this dangerous in business?

Being in business is going to bring to the surface all your beliefs about yourself and what's possible. And if you accept them as unchangeable, then those beliefs will hold you back.

Here's an example of how a belief held me back for almost 10 years in business.

When I left my Wall Street job, I said over and over: "I will never make that much money in my life again. But that's OK because money isn't everything."

I agree money isn't everything. However, having money makes life a whole lot easier. And when you have money, you can have a more significant impact on the world, which was part of what I wanted to do when I left Wall Street. I wanted to do something that would positively affect others.

A few months after quitting my Wall Street job, I started teaching Pilates. And my core perception, coupled with "society's rules," was playing out big time. I was making five times less than I did on Wall Street.

Now you might say: Right, but of course a fitness instructor won't ever earn as much as people on Wall Street. That's just the way it is. Their earning power just isn't the same.

That's what society would like us to believe, but in fact, this common limiting view is totally wrong.

Here are some facts to bust the myth:

Ever heard of the Tone It Up ladies, Katrina Scott and Karena Dawn? They built their multimillion-dollar business starting with an investment of only $3,000 in 2009.[15] (Which, by the way, was right around when I quit my Wall Street job.)

And then there is Cassey Ho, the owner of Blogilates. She is an American social media fitness entrepreneur who started out making one little YouTube fitness video for her friends and grew it into a multimillion-dollar brand.[16]

Never heard of them? I know you'll know the next one: Zumba Fitness. This global workout empire was created by Alberto "Beto" Pérez; he called it "Rumbacize." And later, he partnered with his two other founders, Alberto Perlman and Alberto Aghion, and together the trio released a series of Zumba fitness videos that grew into a sensation.[17]

All of these brands were started a few years before and after I decided to quit my Wall Street career. And they clearly debunk my belief that I couldn't make more than I did on Wall Street.

Quick sidebar: It is important to notice that my earning-power perception was instilled by a limitation that society dictated. It's similar to the "always be humble" South African one or the "starving artist" idea, and it's crucial that you identify ones that your family and your culture have laid out for you as well.

Achieving what you really want will require you to break with mainstream thinking. And this can be very daunting, which is why it's so crucial to get an accountability partner or coach when you first start doing this expansive work.

But let's get back to my beginning years as a fitness instructor: I was constantly saying the words: "I will never make this much money again!" and then repeating them over and over and over again.

Now let's take it back to our Up Level Formula:

Beliefs + Thoughts + Language + Feelings + Actions = Results

It comes as no surprise, then, that my actions were thus heavily impacted by my words, thoughts, and beliefs at the time.

Instead of thinking and dreaming big, I was operating from a constricting place, which led to mediocre ideas that reinforced my faulty thinking. And so my income stayed below my Wall Street salary, even though I worked just as hard, if not more!

I've seen many business owners act from their perceived restrictions as well.

For example:

1. Some entrepreneurs believe that they won't be able to run their business and start a family, so they decide to sell their company. In doing this, they give away the best asset they have to create financial freedom and flexibility on their terms.

2. They don't believe they can build a major business without completely killing themselves in the process. They believe they have to make huge sacrifices to their work-life balance, or put off other life goals and dreams, so they keep their business small (and work themselves to death for very little profit).

But here's the deal: Where there is a will, there's a way. And in the words of Walt Disney: "Whether you believe you can or you can't, you're right."

To build a profitable business that will bring you joy, ease, and high profits, you have to start believing that it's possible.

You don't have to wait 10 years like I did to do this. You can—and should—do it right now.

Debunking those BS beliefs:

1. Grab a piece of paper and write down:

    a. Everything that you believe is impossible for you to achieve

    b. All the things that you believe you're able to accomplish in your business, your life, plus what you deserve.

2. Go through both lists and ask yourself: Why do I think that?

    It's highly likely that you're going to remember a situation similar to mine in my math class or when my teacher cautioned me from working too hard.

3. How did that experience make you feel?

4. Now go further back to the very first time you experienced these feelings.

    Chances are you'll regress to something that happened when you were very little. For me, most of the time, I rewind to age 7, when my best friend told me she no longer wanted to be my BFF.

5. Why was that experience so painful?

    We experience these emotions because a specific need wasn't met.

    Back to my best-friend example: This experience made me feel not good enough to be her friend, and it also left me feeling lonely, like I didn't belong. And I formed a core belief that I don't fit in because I'm not good enough.

You may have to dig deep for this, and it can be quite an emotional exercise. A lot of my clients will try and avoid it for this reason.

But here's the deal: You've committed yourself to do whatever it takes, so now do it. To get to the next level and the expansive version of you, we have to uncover all the underlying beliefs so we can release them and form a new support system in line with what you want.

This process is a little like hardware and software updates. Our thoughts are the software and our beliefs the hardware. To get your computer to run faster and smoother, you need to do both. And the hardware upgrade will ensure that the software upgrades work better too.

Upgrading your belief system:

1. Take that list of beliefs from the previous exercise, and you're going to tap on them. Feel your feelings that come up by speaking them out loud and tapping on them too. Acknowledge them and then release them with love.

    This is a powerful exercise and works a lot like Marie Kondo's "The Life-Changing Magic of Tidying Up." To allow all the exciting new things you want, you have to create space for them. We are creating mental space for fresh, innovative ideas and experiences that will spark excitement.

2. Flip the script.
    Review your list of things you're convinced you can't accomplish. How can you rewrite that narrative?

    Back to my Wall Street example:

    As I mentioned, I believed that I couldn't make more money than I did back then. Flipping that misconception would look something like this:

    I can make as much money as I want to make because I am enough.

    Or

    I'm enough, and it's possible for me to make way more money than I did on Wall Street.

Note: I gave you two very similar examples for a reason. It is important that the flipped statement is something that you really believe. Over time you can adjust it to become more and more daring until it's a limitless mantra of possibility.

Sticking with my previous example, here's how I could amplify it: I build a multimillion-dollar business that supports my health; it's fun and easy.

What we're effectively creating here are mantras. You may also have noticed that they are in the present tense. This is done intentionally to allow you to stop living in the future and create what you want right now.

Debunking, deconditioning, and forming new beliefs are part of an ongoing practice. You can think about it like going to the gym. To obtain and maintain a certain level of fitness, you have to go regularly.

Recipe for success:
It may also be useful to pick one or two beliefs that you actively want to work on, continuously working on reconstructing new supportive and expansive patterns.

This will help you to focus your energy and track your progress while alleviating any overwhelming feelings that may creep in. At the end of each day, you can ask yourself, what were all the things that happened today that support my new belief?

Following this exact process helped me to completely shift what I believed was financially possible for me.

Today I make a similar salary to the one I had on Wall Street in 2008, but unlike when I was on Wall Street, chained to my desk and doing terrible things to my health, I eat three healthy meals that are home-cooked most days, I go for nature walks almost daily, and I love what I do. My business is profitable, and I travel four or five weeks out of the year.

And the best part is that I get to help my clients to do this too. As a result, they have been able to build sustainable and profitable businesses while working less.

When I release my limiting views, I open
myself up to infinite possibility.

Others' opinions never sway my beliefs of
what I can and can't achieve.

I change the beliefs that no longer serve me.

I release all limiting beliefs about
myself and others.

I'm committed to doing whatever it takes.

By changing my limiting thoughts, I also
change the beliefs that are holding me back.

When I release limiting beliefs, I open up
space for fresh ideas and experiences.

1 *Debunking those BS beliefs:*
- *Grab a piece of paper and write down:*

  –Everything that you believe is impossible for you to achieve

  –All the things that you believe you're able to accomplish in your business, your life, plus what you deserve.

- *Go through both lists and ask yourself: Why do I think that?*

- *How did that experience make you feel?*

- *Now go further back to the very first time in your life that you experienced these feelings.*

- *Why was that experience so painful?*

2 *Upgrading your belief system:*
Take that list of beliefs from the previous exercise, and you're going to tap on them. Feel your feelings that come up by speaking them out loud and tapping on them too. Acknowledge them and then release them with love.

3 *Flip the script:*
Review your list of things you're convinced you can't accomplish. How can you rewrite that narrative?

CHAPTER 8:

Be sure to mind your language

Your words have infinite power.

They can empower or disempower you and those around you. And as we've already seen from our Up Level Formula, your words play a huge part in accomplishing your goals.

Beliefs + Thoughts + **Language** + Feelings + Actions = Results

---

It's impossible for you to create a successful business that brings you joy and happiness if your words are not aligned with that goal.

As coaches, we're trained to listen for these misalignments. Our words are a window into our soul, what we think, and what we believe. And that's why I can have a five-minute conversation with someone and tell you how likely it is that they'll accomplish their goal.

Let's revisit what I initially said about leaving my Wall Street job, which led to me feeling convinced that I'd never make that kind of big money again.

If you were listening to me with a trained ear, you'd be able to deduce the following:

- she has a broken/limited relationship with money
- she is insecure about her abilities and money
- she is constricting her own earning potential

These were all things I believed to be true. Of course, the Wall Street circles that I traveled in then were also conditioned to think in a similar way and thus reinforced my beliefs.

This is often why it's so hard for people to break the vicious cycle because our communities will often mirror those limitations for us.

30 seconds to improve your mood:
Yes, let's go all California style on things for a second. Stick with me; you're going to love this exercise.

One of my first business coaches introduced me to the work of Esther Hicks, often ascribed to Abraham Hicks. She is an American inspirational speaker and author who co-wrote nine books with her late husband, Jerry Hicks. Esther also presented numerous workshops on the law of attraction with Abraham Hicks Publications and appeared in the 2006 movie "The Secret."[18]

Specifically, my coach gave me an exercise that is similar to one Esther Hicks talks about quite often. And it works great when one's mind is in the gutter. And it goes like this: For 30 seconds straight, you repeat positive statements out loud to yourself.

For example, you could say the following:

I'm a great leader.
My business is a Fortune 500 company.
I have the best marriage.
My kids are amazingly resourceful and find their way in the world.
I make money fast and easy.
And so on.

You can also do it by starting with the words "what if" and then go into a positive statement. This helps it to feel more possible and helps your brain to believe the statement.
Such as:

What if I build a Fortune 500 company...?
What if I make money fast and easy...?

The idea is that you do this for half a minute, and it will elevate your mood, so you feel better. It, of course, syncs perfectly with the Up Level Formula too. Incorporating this exercise will improve all parts of the equation, including your results.

Anyhow, at the time, I was newer to my coaching business and was really trying to get my name out there.

So between sessions, I would repeat the following to myself:

What if I became a renowned business coach?
What if I got amazing new clients every week?
What if I had X amount of participants in my class tonight?

I did this every single day for months. In fact, I still play this game all the time.

A while later, after practicing this routine, I received an email from Boston Magazine. It had just announced its Best of Boston Awards, and guess who was awarded the best life coach? Yep, that would be me, yours truly over here.

I was so shocked. I thought it might be a spam email. It wasn't. I had received this prestigious award fair and square and only one and a half years into starting my coaching business.

You bet I celebrated the heck out of this one!

Using that 30-second exercise helped me to build trust in myself, and as a result, I showed up more confidently in my business too. And that confidence led me to pitch some stories to Boston Magazine, which then invited me to be on a panel.

I was on the radar of one of the best magazines in the U.S. That's me, a girl from a tiny little town, with only two streets, in South Africa. And the reason I got there in the first place was that I played that game. I paid attention to my words.

I changed my language, and it won me an esteemed award!

So trust me when I say: your words have so much freaking power over you, who you become, and what you achieve.

If you have difficulty figuring out or tracking your thoughts, paying attention to your words might be an easier way to build awareness.

When I work with my clients, I'll help them to become mindful of their language. I'll stop them mid-sentence or go "ah!" as a pattern interrupter. It's incredible to watch them catch themselves in our sessions and correct their own language once we've been working together for a while.

We also take time to Google the meaning of words, thus providing them with language to fully express themselves.

And, of course, what's so beautiful to watch is how their confidence soars and their results grow! They gain more clarity on what they want, they start to see the map to get there, and they're able to better lead their team in a more direct way.

The first agreement in the classic personal-development book "The Four Agreements: A Practical Guide to Personal Freedom," written by Don Miguel Ruiz with Janet Mills, is: "Be impeccable with your speech."[19]

I couldn't agree more.

So let's take a little deeper dive into the words that you want to pay particular attention to:

Are you using words that are not definitive and concise? Here are some offending words:

- Try
- Maybe
- Guess
- Perhaps

These words all indicate that you don't believe you can accomplish something, or don't trust the situation/process, or yourself, and/or are not committed to whatever you say after. They are giving you an out. They are not the words of a determined person.

Using these words will give you so-so results. Replace them with more committed expressions like:

- I am going to do
- I can
- I will

Then there are words that create more pressure like:

- Need
- Must
- Should

These words indicate that you're trying to control or are judging yourself and/or others.

Think of words that are more freeing and will relieve some of the pressure:

- I can/want vs. need
- I am allowed to; I'm open to doing it vs. must
- I will/want to vs. should

There are many more examples of words you're using that are not in alignment with what you want, but alas, we can't cover them all here, so here's a quick check that you can do with yourself:

When thinking about goals/results you want, ask yourself if the statements and words you're saying are serving that goal. Is your language clear and concise? Are you using definitive language?

Remember: Your words have infinite power, so choose them wisely!

I use empowering words to inspire myself
and others.

When I change my words to align with what I
want to attain, magic happens.

I'm impeccable with my speech.

My words have infinite power,
I choose them wisely.

UP LEVEL IT NOW:

1 *Becoming more intentional and aligned with your words: what offending words are you currently aware of using? What committed language can you use instead?*

Recap of offending words:
- *Try*
- *Maybe*
- *Guess*
- *Perhaps*

Recap of committed expressions:
- *I am going to do*
- *I can*
- *I will*

2 *Where have you noticed yourself using words that create pressure? What freeing words can you use instead?*

Recap of words that create more pressure:
- *Need*
- *Must*
- *Should*

Recap of words that will relieve some of the pressure:
- *I can/want vs. need*
- *I am allowed to; I'm open to doing it vs. must*
- *I will/want to vs. should*

3 *Think of one or two goals that you are working toward. Write out a few sentences that use committed and or freeing language aligned with what you want to achieve.*

CHAPTER 9:

Are you unknowingly sabotaging yourself?

Next up to get the results you want is to take a look at your actions and, more important, how everything prior in our Up Level Formula influences our actions. (Don't worry, I didn't forget about feelings, which we'll get to in Chapter 10.)

Beliefs + Thoughts + Language + Feelings + **Actions** = Results

---

Once you've aligned all of the previous steps, you'll usually be able to take massive, aligned, and inspired action. You'll be excited to leap forward (most of the time).

Sometimes, however, your actions may be toxic and sabotaging. And this usually happens right after you've broken through to a new level of prosperity and abundance, such as landing the most profitable client contract you've ever had. Why?

To get to the bottom of why I have to come clean with you. Throughout my career, I've had a dirty little habit that would rear its ugly head just as I was doing really well.

It got particularly bad once I started my Pilates business. I had built my company up, with a loyal following, to award-winning status within two years. I could see myself being the next Jane Fonda! I had already produced a few fitness DVDs. What would be next?!

I was on a high; nothing could stop me. Or so I thought. And then my good old sabotaging friend paid me a visit, as it always did.

I started to look around and compared myself to others in my industry. I began to view them as my competition, something or someone I had to prove that I was better than. You can imagine the negative self-talk that this would stir up. All of it was happening so I could prove my old belief true, the one that felt familiar and comfy: "See, I told you so—you're not good enough." Comparing myself with others robbed me of any faith I had in myself.

This thought pattern threw me off and influenced the action I was taking. Instead of doing what made me happy, and fulfilling *my* dreams, I was doing things to "keep up with the Joneses" of the Pilates world.

Taking action from that frame of mind led to making less money and having less fun. Looking back at it now, I could have accomplished so much more if I had not let that sabotaging behavior run the show. Instead, I ended up doing lots of things that weren't aligned with who I was, and I finally burnt out to such a degree that teaching Pilates was no longer enjoyable.

Everything that I had worked so hard for since quitting Wall Street—earning my certification, building relationships with the most amazing and loyal clients, getting publicity, making and selling DVDs, winning an award—it all got flushed down the toilet.

It was around this time something else happened as well. I heard through the grapevine that one particular person who I saw as competition was bad-mouthing me rather publicly. (Looks like I wasn't the only one feeling a little jealous.)

And that was it, the final straw. I was so done! Because my other sabotaging behavior is: I run away from drama.

Now you may ask yourself: "But isn't that a positive tactic?"

Yes, it is, when you state your boundaries and make yourself unavailable for such drama. But in my case, instead of ignoring the theatrics, I usually cut my losses and run—and apologize for taking up space while doing so.

Makes me think of that saying, "When the going gets tough, the tough get going," except in my case, it was more like, "When the going gets tough, the tough start running."

I had done this in high school when girls got mean, I did this on Wall Street, and here I was doing it again. Every time I did it, I lost a little piece of myself. I made myself smaller and smaller to avoid the drama, slowly chipping away my confidence.

The losses were more than just emotional opportunities to grow and get stronger. Running away from the drama impacted me financially too.

I didn't address the theatrics head-on because I believed that I was inadequate. And that belief robbed me of expressing myself and using all my talents and gifts. And that impacted my ability to create a financially abundant life.

So why was this happening?

Both my competitive behavior and aversion to drama kept me from being too amazing or becoming too successful. My subconscious mind saw being too wonderful as bad and wrong.

Let's go deeper into why this happens.

In his book "The Big Leap: Conquer Your Hidden Fear and Take Life to the Next Level," Gay Hendricks[20] explains that we have four zones that we typically operate in:

1. Incompetence: The stuff that's really not in your wheelhouse of strengths, where you don't shine/excel at all—the zone where you're not your best self.

2. Competence: The zone of stuff you can do, but you're not that great and doesn't light you up. This is the zone where you're just an OK version of yourself.

3. Excellence: This is the zone where you operate most of the time, where you're just good enough to fit in, not too loud, not overly ambitious, where everything is just right (but you're not living up to your full potential). This is also the zone where you're a better version of yourself, but not the Porsche version. You're more like a Kia: reliable, middle-class, looks nice enough. (FYI, I love Kias—my hubby drives one!)

4. Genius: The zone where you're living and doing the things that truly light you up, where you're using all your gifts to your fullest potential. This is the zone where you're the best possible version of yourself. In this version, you're taking up space, you're bold, and you don't mind standing out or ruffling a few feathers.

As an entrepreneur, I know that you're drooling all over the Genius zone right now. That's the place where you strive to be. That's where you belong. That's what I was aiming for when I started my Pilates business too.

In "The Big Leap," Hendricks also notes that our fears and beliefs usually prevent us from operating in that zone. We'll see glimpses of it, like when you destroy that sales call and sign the biggest contract of your life, or when you have a super good meeting with your staff where you are not afraid to have those tough conversations, have a week of being completely organized and getting everything on your to-do list done. There are days and weeks that you're nailing it! You feel fantastic, you feel confident, you feel like you're a freaking god/goddess!

This is where I was when I won that award that recognized me as one of Boston's most innovative companies. I was on top of the freaking world. I felt like nothing or no one could stop me. I felt like I was invincible, and I could accomplish everything.

And then boom! You have a fight of the century with your partner. Or you have a few glasses of vino too many at dinner, and you have the worst hangover the next day and can't do a thing. Or, in my case, you start competing with others.

All of a sudden, you're right back to feeling like you're not enough, small and insignificant, and you're grumpy, and that high you felt a few days prior is nowhere to be found.

You've been pulled back down to what Hendricks calls the zones of competence or excellence. This happens because our subconscious mind is trying to protect us. Our fears and beliefs are pulling us back to the OK version of us because we believe it's bad or wrong to be that amazing all the time.

We have been conditioned with things like:

- Bad things usually happen in threes.

- When things go this well, something terrible always follows.

- Blow out your candles, and make a wish—but don't tell anyone; otherwise, the wish won't come true.

- Don't be a tall poppy. (My American friends: that means don't be too big for your boots.)

- No one likes a bragger.

- Rich people are evil.

- Money is dirty.

The list goes on. And on.

When we break down these sayings to their core, we'll get to your safety. Everything on this list is designed to help you survive and keep you from experiencing negative consequences.

When we become aware of these behaviors, we see them for what they are: big freaking distractions. They are bumps in the road that are keeping us from what we truly want!

And when we can identify our distracting behaviors, we can stop them from happening or stop them while they're happening. We can pump the brakes before they let us burn down businesses, micro-manage our staff or not give them direction at all, get into nasty arguments, or drink too much and have that super unproductive hangover.

We can trace back where these habits came from, and we can deconstruct the belief that fuels them and heal the wound that it has created within us. And the great news is that you can also use this exact process when you're finding yourself in limbo or resisting to take action, or doing the exact opposite of what you say you want to create.

When we want to achieve our goals, aligned action is key to realizing our desires.

You're a warrior, and you're on your way to greatness. It is possible for you to be in your zone of genius and achieve all the success you want. All you need to do is stop shooting yourself in the foot with all these bad habits that go directly against what you want.

I spot my behavioral patterns that sabotage
my success and change them effortlessly.

I choose to act in ways that support the
results I want.

I realize my dreams through aligned action.

1 *What are your sabotaging behaviors?*

2 *What are the things that you have done after big
wins that took you in the opposite direction of where you
want to go?*

3 *Come up with a few actions that will interrupt
your knee-jerk reactions. E.g. Whenever you want to go to
your competitors' Instagram to compare yourself to them,
look up testimonials from your happy clients instead.*

4 *Go back to Chapter 7 and uncover what beliefs
are causing you to act out and then deconstruct and
release them.*

CHAPTER 10:

Feel it to achieve it and supercharge the Up Level Formula

W hile reading Denise Duffield-Thomas' book "Get Rich, Lucky Bitch!: Release Your Money Blocks and Live a First-Class Life," I stumbled across a quote that made me laugh out loud:

"Like farts, goals are better out than in; so stop bottling them up and let them into the world." [21]

Tell me that made you smile, if not laugh out loud. The thing is, this quote applies to your feelings too. Let's read that quote replacing goals with feelings:

"Like farts, feelings are better out than in."

Think for a moment about the last time you were about to cry in public. Remember that moment where your eyes started to water? You swallowed, blinked hard, and tried to push those tears right back into your tear ducts. But they pushed back, harder, and more determined to be let out into the world. And for a split second, you thought you were going to lose the battle and break down sobbing.

That's how all your emotions respond when you bottle them up and push them down. Bottling up your feelings means that they'll revolt.

And when we take a look at our Up Level Formula:

Beliefs + Thoughts + Language + **Feelings** + Actions = Results

From my crying example above, we can clearly see that when your emotions fight back hard, they will cause a distraction or disruption to the results you want.

Most people's natural reaction is to get upset for feeling a certain un-desired emotion. We condemn it and are hard on ourselves. When we this, our inner child starts throwing tantrums, feeling ignored and unheard. And before we know it, we're having a full-blown meltdown.

As the word clearly implies: Feelings are meant to be felt. Feeling a feeling means you acknowledge its existence. Yet most of us do not allow ourselves to do that. Instead, we shove those emotions into various corners of our bodies.

Of course, the messaging around a so-called "positive mindset" and self-coaching models that flood our society don't help either. We've been conditioned to think that to achieve success we must have a positive mindset and always feel happy, fun feelings.

Most of us were raised by parents who were raised by parents who didn't have the luxury of processing and exploring their feelings. Our grandparents lived during the Great Depression and World War II. In those days, to survive—and what was expected of you—was to put your feelings aside and get on with it.

It's no wonder that so many of us, then, have such a tough time processing our emotions. We've all been told at various points in our life, when we've been upset or experienced negative emotions, to "not feel that way."

Dr. Abigail Brenner brings up an interesting fact about the words "motion" and "emotion." According to Dr. Brenner: "Movere, from the Latin, means to move. Exmovere or emovere means to move out, hence to excite. So taking action stirs something up, moves something inside of us."

No wonder she titled that particular article, "E~motions of Change = Energy in Motion."[22]

Continuing with that thought, another mentor of mine, Suzy Ashworth, a mindset and business coach, likes to quote one of Albert Einstein's famous sayings that further proves just how ineffective it is to suppress your emotions.

"Energy cannot be created or destroyed. It can only be changed from one form to another," Einstein said.

And that's probably why it feels so good to punch something when you're angry. You're taking that emotion, moving it through your body and into your fist, and POW! A release.

When we push our feelings into deep little corners of our body, two things happen:

1. Our feelings get stuck and can cause serious illnesses.[23]

2. We miss valuable information that our feelings are trying to give us.

It's for these very reasons that I often ask my clients to describe, in detail, where a specific emotion is presenting itself and how they're experiencing it in their body.

Most people tend to get lodged in their minds, overthinking and feeling too little, and as a result, they stay in limbo, unable to take action.

Knowing, feeling, and accepting your emotions will allow them to move through you while giving you great feedback on what to do to feel better. Step aside and let those feelings run free.

When you do this, you invite space to get curious about the experience. And when you take a closer look, you'll most likely figure out that you're feeling a particular way because of certain thoughts or beliefs you have. If that's the case, you can actively interrupt those patterns to have a different experience altogether.

I remember the first client who broke a contract with me with no explanation. I was shocked because up to that point, the client had been seeing great results from our work together and was so excited about their progress.

When I reminded them of my termination clause—which states that when you cancel the contract, you are still liable for the full cost of the program—they got agitated and attacked my character.

I immediately felt a range of emotions:

- Confused and hurt by their attack

- Annoyed and angry that they could conduct business this way

- And fear: what if they bad-mouthed me? What if I never got any other clients again?

As with most of us, my first reaction was to make myself feel better. I wanted to do something to make it all go away, and, of course, all those negative emotions pushed back harder and with more fury.

And so I surrendered. I allowed myself to feel it all. I meditated on it, did tapping (EFT—the Emotional Freedom Technique I taught you in

Chapter 6), and journaled. I sought advice from a friend who's a lawyer and vented to my hubby about it.

Throughout the process, I allowed myself to be curious: What's the story I'm telling myself about how this reflects on me, and my character, my business?

Here's what I told myself: I was mean; I was a horrible person for enforcing the clause.

I followed all the clues and went deeper by asking myself: And why am I feeling this way?

When I listened and assessed all the messages my body sent me, it came down to the same belief that we've heard several times in this book: "I'm not enough."

Once I understood that this belief was triggering all those feelings, I was able to trace this pattern back to other experiences that had happened in my life as well. This helped me to break the behavior down even further.

And here's what I uncovered:

When I draw a firm boundary and stand up for what I believe to be fair, and I then get a negative response from the person I'm drawing the line with, I tend to go into self-criticizing mode. I make myself out to be the "bad" one who's not worthy of having her needs met. So instead of honoring my values, I'll compromise and profusely start apologizing.

This leads to a ton of conflicting emotions:

- Anger, because I'm ignoring the part of me that stands for my values

- Fear, because I'm scared of what others will think of me

And my immediate reaction is to act from that place of fear. Which meant in this instance, I wanted to start apologizing, let them out of the contract, and do anything to get the client's approval and tell me that everything is cool. And that would make me feel like I'm enough.

But that's not what my business needed from me here. When you allow your emotions to run you and your business, they will cause havoc.

As you know by now, your business requires you to do a whole lot of things that are not always pleasant and don't feel easy. It requires you to look at the data, to think about what is required of you for your business to grow and survive. It requires you to act from your values and the business' needs.

This is exactly why it's so important to have certain structures and protocols in place that will support you in these situations.

I'm running a business, and I have contracts in place to create a safe and trustworthy space for both my clients and for myself.

By signing a contract, clients agree to and know what service they'll receive, along with the peace of mind that we're entering into a confidential relationship. And they know that I'll be there to support them.

And for my business, a contract also provides financial security, which means that I can show up to sessions fully present without worrying about money.

Of course, I appreciate that many things can happen that might impact the ability to enforce the contract to its full extent. When that happens, I'm available and willing to have a conversation about a solution that will honor and work well for both parties, even if that's a difficult discussion to have.

That's ultimately the value and space I decided to act from. It wasn't easy, and it didn't feel comfortable. Often what is required of you won't be the thing that you feel like doing, but you'll have to do it anyway.

Through this example, we can clearly see how I used my emotions to gain two valuable insights:

1. I pinpointed a disempowering belief.

2. My feelings highlighted how I was about to act out of alignment.

This awareness further guided me on the next steps that my business needed me to take. I pursued a lawyer to remedy the situation. It felt so good to know that I upheld my ethics. And it taught me that I'll be able to step up and handle any difficult situation in the future.

If you can cultivate your awareness of how and where feelings manifest in your body and what they are trying to tell you, you can make them work in your favor.

This brings us to the next point:

Supercharging the Up Level Formula:

What makes the Up Level Formula stand out is this: I include language as an indicator to make it easier to identify what's going on in your mind and help increase your awareness around beliefs, thoughts, and behaviors that lead to undesired outcomes.

Up to this point, I used it as a linear equation. However, our mind tends to work in circles and spirals.

The Up Level Formula also flows in a circular motion, creating a constant feedback loop for us. At the core of that loop are our beliefs influencing our words, our thoughts, our feelings, and our actions.

And when we pay close enough attention, we're able to spot (and interrupt) the patterns that hold us back from creating our deepest desires and biggest dreams. We can trace it all back to whatever limiting belief is causing the misalignment to happen.

It is also important to remember that this work is like peeling an onion. Every time you reach a new level of growth and abundance, there will be another layer to peel back and explore, much like my example of the broken contract. Through our behaviors and experiences, we grow and expand into new versions of ourselves. And wishing for these conditions to always be perfect is essentially wishing away what it means to be human.

This brings us to another important point: trying to be perfect.

You do not have to perfect every aspect of the Up Level Formula to achieve better results. All you need to do is incrementally up-level it. That's why I called it the Up Level Formula and not the Get It Perfect Equation.

Building your awareness of the components of the Up Level Formula and systematically upgrading parts of it while lovingly accepting where you are, despite any flaws, will open you up to massive personal growth, joy, ease, and abundance.

Like my farts, feelings are better out than in.

Feeling and accepting my emotions allow them to move through me, causing less pain.

My feelings give me great feedback on what to do to feel better.

My business structures and protocols are set up to support me when facing difficult situations.

My feelings are always giving me valuable insight.

Through my behaviors and experiences, I grow and expand into new versions of myself.

I'm grateful for all my feelings, good and bad.

**UP LEVEL
IT NOW:**

1 *Where and how do you experience negative emotion in your body? Think about where precisely you feel it and how it feels.*

- *Get curious about that feeling—does it feel heavy, constricting, painful?*

- *Do you feel it in your head, your shoulders, chest, stomach?*

- *Get as specific as possible here.*

2 *Next time you're triggered:*

- *Practice accepting the feeling by breathing into it. You can even say to yourself: "I accept feeling X." Notice what happens.*

- *What story are you telling yourself about the feeling?*

- *What are you making this story mean about yourself?*

- *Where does this story come from?*

- *What else is the feeling trying to tell you?*

3 *Listen to an interview I did with Suzy Ashworth, mindset and business coach, about how using many of the principles we discussed in the last few chapters, helped her to quadruple her income in record time. Access the interview by visiting: hannekeantonelli.com/book-bonus*

CHAPTER 11:

The one thing that will derail and delay your progress

D uring my coaching certification, I discovered something that fascinated me.

I've already told you how anxious I used to be, and for years I would wake up in the middle of the night with my heart racing and pounding. Nervous, sweaty, scared. I'm pretty sure those were anxiety attacks. As a result of my physical discomfort, my brain would immediately go into a tailspin asking why? Why are you so anxious? Why am I experiencing this? Why? Why? Why?

I also remember asking that question when I was doing things I knew were sabotaging my progress. Or I'd ask, "Why is this happening to me? Why am I not able to do X?" and these questions would inevitably lead to "what is wrong with me?" followed by another "why can't I...?"

And so it would go on and on and on, creating more and more panic. I know I'm not the only person who does this. In my coaching practice, I have seen most of my clients do the same.

As coaches, we're always interested in forward motion and action toward our clients' desired outcome. We spend less time unpacking the past and more time bringing clients back to the present moment.

We believe that the answer to every challenge and problem lies within the client already. And our job is to uncover that wisdom by the process of positive inquiry. Certified coaches are trained to listen on multiple levels and be extremely curious during sessions.

Based on what we hear, we'll ask our clients lots of questions and reflect back to them what we are hearing and noticing. Our questions almost always start with what, how, when, who, where, and hardly ever with why.

By carefully asking those questions, based on what my clients are saying and what I'm hearing and noticing, I help them to uncover their truth and solve overwhelming situations. Once they have their solution, it's easier for them to take inspired action in service of their goals.

But when we ask "why," it does the opposite.

Trained and certified coaches will refrain from asking clients "why" questions because they tend to keep clients stuck in the past. It deliberately keeps them spinning in circles about what has already happened instead of what they want going forward. It creates a vicious cycle of blame and shame.

"Why" questions also have an accusatory feel to them. And they immediately put the person to whom you're asking the question on the defense. By asking someone "why?" you immediately let them feel like they did something wrong.

Why did you tell the client that?
Why would you say something like that?
Why am I doing this to myself?
Why did you cheat on me?

By asking yourself why, you're taking a magnifying glass to a situation, expanding it, and then get completely stuck in it, fueling feelings of humiliation and guilt. And as a result, you're unable to work on a constructive outcome.

On a related note: This is also very important to remember when you're working with your staff.

Replace why questions with what, when, where, how, and who questions when talking to your employees. This will help you effectively communicate with your staff in a more constructive way that's solution-driven and inspires action.

So if asking why is such a sticky question, why do we keep asking it?

The answer is simple: Your brain is always looking to understand the world within and around you. It's always trying to figure out what's going on so it can make decisions on how to keep you safe and alive. This is, of course, your brain's primary function, and also known as the fight-or-flight response. The part of your brain that regulates this function is an almond-shaped structure that is situated in the temporal lobe and called the amygdala.[24]

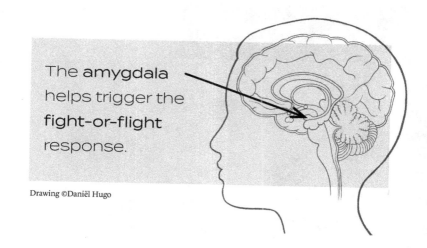

The **amygdala** helps trigger the **fight-or-flight** response.

Drawing ©Daniël Hugo

Unfortunately, we may never understand why you do something or feel the way you do.

After all, some of what you're dealing with might be generational conditioning or things that happened to you before you were able to understand them on a conscious level.

To inspire forward motion, it's essential to stop dwelling on why and start asking yourself what, where, how, when and with whom instead.

Set yourself free from the blame and shame of your behaviors, and commit to creating forward momentum instead.

I move toward a solution by focusing on what, when, who, and where.

When I focus on what I want, the how always reveals itself.

I inspire forward motion by not dwelling on why.

I set myself free from my past behaviors and commit to creating forward momentum instead.

1 *Notice where you're getting stuck in a "why?" spiral that results in blame and shame.*

2 *Instead of why, start asking yourself where, what, who, when, how.*

THE UP LEVEL PROJECT

Preparing for Takeoff

12. Letting go of fitting in

13. A leader is born

14. Achieving more while doing less

15. Have a little faith... in yourself

CHAPTER 12:

Letting go of fitting in

The road to extraordinary can often be lonely, one where you feel out of sorts and displaced, like you don't belong.

Growing up, I was often the odd one out.

I was the only girl in my family and the youngest of the kids, trailing my brothers by four and seven years. Being this much younger meant I had to grow up a whole lot faster than other kids so I could fit into what is the most important place in your world when you're little: family.

Most little girls' Barbies would be living with Ken in their castle. Not my Barbies. Mine had Ken as their sergeant major. That's right: my Barbies were in the army! They had backpacks that my brother constructed out of cardboard and sleeping bags that my mom sewed for us.

Those were also the days of the TV series "Highlander," and the three of us would have lots of sword fights, using sticks as our make-believe dragon-head katana. Boldly announcing that "There can be only one!" I was usually not that one.

If I slipped and fell while playing or got hurt because my brothers were too rough, I'd usually get a big hug, which was more like a firm hold so I couldn't run to my mom and get them in trouble. My middle brother would always say to me: "You're OK, don't cry—you're a big girl!"

I firmly believe that part of why I've accomplished half of the things I've done in my life is because these two taught me how to be strong, resilient, creative, savvy, and a go-getter.

But when I was a kid, fitting in with my older siblings posed a challenge when playing with kids my own age. I had learned to stand my ground and was thus perceived as bossy. At PTA meetings, the feedback would always be: Hanneke presents much older than her peers, and that is making it a little harder for her socially.

Being an outsider who had a deep desire to fit in meant that I spent most of my life compromising parts of my personality. And the truth is, trying to fit in wasn't working that well anyway. All it did was make me feel more out of place, further feeding the idea that I was somehow flawed.

Just like you, I have certain strengths and certain weaknesses. I have unique gifts. And we both have a different purpose to fulfill, a particular role to play. Trying to fit in diminishes and robs us of everything that will bring us joy and help us become our most confident and peaceful selves.

Unfortunately, we don't have this knowledge when we're at the most impressionable stages of life. And so tenaciously, like any other kid, including you, I kept trying my damndest to fit in.

Here are a few scenarios where I tried to belong and failed, leaving me with that lonely displaced feeling:

- At school, I tried to be all chill, but I was the serious one and the nerd.

- In England and America, I was, and still remain, the one with the accent.

- And for a very long time, while running my Pilates business, I used my accent as a crutch, a reason why I would never be as popular or successful as others.

Of course, that's a load of nonsense. You may already know by now that when running a business, leaning into and amplifying all the things that make you different is precisely what will make you stand out and attract your ideal clients faster.

It's time to stop hiding.

It's time to stop caring what your parents, your team, your friends, and the world will think.

It's time to step boldly into all the gifts that make you unique.

Easy as pie, right?

No.

Here's why you haven't done it yet. Taking that massive leap means that you'll have to go against the grain.

Fully expressing yourself and what you really think, feel, and have accomplished means that you won't fit in. And that right there is scary. Because that could mean that you'll end up being all alone.

That's also why so many people won't commit to working at and implementing the processes and strategies in this book.

When you start to do the work to gain clarity, to remove all the things that are keeping you stuck, unfulfilled, and preventing you from growing your business to its most glorious capacity, you won't fit in with the status quo.

In practice, this means that you'll be the one at social gatherings who says, when asked, that things are going amazing in your business, despite the three people who answered this question before you saying their business is not doing well.

And you'll be the one who shows up at your staff meetings ready to lead, unafraid to have courageous conversations, and not place so much value on having to be liked all the time.

You'll be the one who doesn't engage in the gossip.

You'll be the one who no longer wants to hang out with people who are constantly criticizing themselves and judging others harshly.

Most people are afraid to do the aforementioned, and I get why.

But the real question for you is this: What is all this trying to fit in and not rocking the boat costing you?

There's a saying that you are the average of the five people you spend most of your time with.

- Who are those five for you right now?

- Is conforming to their standards really worth never living up to your fullest potential and experiencing all the abundance, joy, and ease that are available to you?

- And when you're really honest with yourself, is this really giving you the desired feelings of belonging and being understood?

I'll answer those questions for you: It's not.

That fear of losing friends and being unpopular and alone is a bunch of crap.

How do I know this with so much certainty? You're already lonely because you're denying yourself the very thing that will give you a sense of affinity: self-acceptance.

Also, I've moved countries multiple times, and I naturally lost a few friends along the way. But I've never been without, at least, one good friend.

And here's one of the best things that happened as a result of moving around so much:

- I had to learn to accept myself and have my own back. And miraculously, it became easier to release people who caused drama, were negative Nancies, couldn't get out of their own way, and didn't cheer me on.

- Allowing myself to own my singular traits has filled my life with the most amazing people.

This doesn't mean that I'm not there for friends who are going through hard stuff. On the contrary, I have many friends who have had to face and overcome harsh obstacles. The difference, however, is this: These are friends who are also continually working on growing, and expanding, and becoming better versions of themselves. They're taking an active role in their quest for excellence. We don't allow ourselves to get stuck and sink.

Surrounding yourself with supportive, high-achieving friends doesn't mean the road won't get rocky. It does, however, mean that you'll still be able to cheer them on even when you're eating dirt or the other way around. And seeing them do inspiring things will help you to spit out the dirt and try again. You'll fuel one another and push one another to become the best versions of yourselves.

In all my moving around, I've also realized that the saying that some people come for a reason, a season, or a lifetime is true.

When you run a business, you're most likely going to find yourself outgrowing a lot of people along the way. Note that this doesn't make you better or worse than someone else. We're all here to learn from one another and to blossom. And that growth will take some of us on a similar path and life experience, and others on a different one. And it's all good.

You're on a different path than most. You've chosen the road of entrepreneurship because you were looking for something different than the norm. You wanted a life that would allow you an extraordinary experience. So stop trying to have that white picket fence.

Stepping into your remarkable life requires you to release all the things and people who no longer serve you and are not in alignment with the abundance you crave.

When you finally allow yourself to stand out from the pack and step into your uncommon strength, you'll be amazed by the wonderful friends and customers you'll gain (not to mention the impact and inspiration you'll give others!).

Added bonus: When you allow yourself to become that fully expressed version of you, your confidence will soar! You will stop second-guessing yourself, and clarity will naturally come to you because you'll be firmly and boldly standing in your truth.

You'll become your most magnetic and powerful self.

And finally, those feelings of not fitting in will be replaced by a deep sense of satisfaction and belonging.

I'm here to fulfill my unique purpose;
I surround myself with people who cheer
me on!

The more I lean into my authentic self, the
more confidence and peace I experience.

It's natural to outgrow certain people;
we're all here for different reasons.

It's safe for me to break with the status quo
and choose extraordinary experiences.

With love, I release all the people who, and
things that, are no longer in alignment with the
abundance I desire.

Leading with my unique strengths attracts
extraordinary people and opportunities.

When I act from my highest self, I create
a ripple effect of inspiration, positively
impacting others.

When I stand in my truth, I am a clear and
decisive leader.

**UP LEVEL
IT NOW:**

1 *Who are the people in your life who cheer you on?*

2 *Who are the people whom you try to fit in with?*

3 *Who are the people with whom you have stimulating conversations?*

4 *Who are the people whose conversations leave you depleted/feeling bad about yourself?*

CHAPTER 13:

A leader is born

A music teacher once told me I was an idiot.

That's right. During our session, I was doing some scale runs, and I kept getting stuck at this one particular spot. Now, I'm fully aware of how annoying it is to sit and listen to someone practicing piano (or any instrument, for that matter), especially if they keep tripping up in the same place over and over again.

And so, on my next try, when I stumbled at that exact spot again, my teacher said something along the lines of:

"Oh, come on, you idiot...."

I was so shocked I didn't get the rest of her sentence. I was only 16 years old. Hearing this from a teacher, someone who is supposed to encourage students, crushed my spirit. It took everything I had not to burst into tears and lose my cool right there. I finished up the session and kept thinking about what had just happened.

I was one of the most hard-working, diligent students she had. I practiced piano for 45 minutes every day, despite having a very full schedule with ballet and living in the boarding school where it was often difficult to access a piano. How dare she call me an idiot?

I had heard her do similar things to other students too. Something had to be done. But what?

The good thing about living in a boarding school starting at age 14 is that it makes you super self-sufficient and independent. You learn to stand up for yourself and fight your own battles real fast because your parents aren't there to step in.

So instead of running to my mom and getting her to call the headmaster and report this teacher, I decided to speak to her myself.

Needless to say that I was very nervous about doing it. What if she exploded again? She had such a bad temper. I took a left down the long small corridor down a couple of steps to her office. My heart was pounding. My palms were sweaty. But I continued to walk with determination. I knocked on the door, and I heard her say that I could enter.

I stood by the door and asked if now was a good time to speak with her about something.

It was.

I wasted no time and immediately got to the point. I told her that I felt her words were out of line, that she knew that I was one of her most dedicated students whose homework was always done, and that I was always prepared for sessions. I was trying my very best. And for that reason, I didn't think that it was fair or appropriate to call me—or any of her students—an idiot. I held my breath...

She looked at me for a second, which felt like a minute.

I could see that she was a little startled and flushed. She usually did this when she was about to explode, which made me brace inside. But then her expression became clear—she was blushing because she was embarrassed.

I'm pretty sure no kid had ever called her out on her inappropriate behavior. I kept standing tall in the doorway.

After what felt like an eternity, she said she was sorry.

It had taken everything I had to muster up the courage to go and speak to her, so I was eager to get out of her office and didn't stay to make small talk. I got what I came for.

Just like that, I had stood up for myself. A thousand-pound weight lifted off my shoulders.

I walked back through the long, dark hallway, my head high. Vindicated. Liberated. It was the very same feeling I had the day I was done confronting my rapist.

Relief.

Exactly the feeling I had when I was walking out of my Wall Street boss' office after calling out all the sexually inappropriate behavior and harassment I had felt in my workplace. Speaking my truth had set me free.

Sure, boarding school, traveling, and my work had made me super versatile, and I could be fluid and fit in anywhere. But I could never diminish my morals and values to fit into a confined box. I've never been able to be silent when I saw something that my core believed to be wrong.

Suddenly, I had proof that when I speak my truth, good things happen. I become a leader, and I lead boldly and bravely.

It's easy to forget that you're a leader when you're a business owner. After all, when you started your business, you were so occupied with your passion for the project and caught up in making it profitable.

Your intention may never have been to lead. But that's what you inevitably become in the process of scaling and growing your business and team. And as we're all becoming more attuned to social justice, now more than ever, it's crucial that your company reflects the impact you want to have on the world.

All of this means that you'll have to lead with your values.

And much like me, it means that you'll have to speak up for what you believe in, have those difficult conversations, and draw boundaries of what is and what's not acceptable. If you want to grow a sustainable and profitable business, you'll need to step up and guide your team and your customers too. Without your stewardship, your company's culture will crumble, your employees will grow increasingly frustrated, and that will directly impact your bottom line. Happy employees increase profits.

Clients often get haunted by imposter syndrome about leadership. After all, how could they be leaders if they never went to business school or never received leadership training?

I remind them that President Abraham Lincoln also didn't go to Leadership 101. In fact, he had very little formal education, yet he practiced law for 17 years and became one of the best trial attorneys in the state of Illinois. And later, he led America through one of its most trying times, the Civil War. Partly as a result of his leadership, slavery was abolished.[25]

Again: he had no college education! He was what we refer to as a QBE: Qualified by Experience. And he wasn't scared of standing up to defend his beliefs and values that would better the lives of others.

And this is what you are too: You're a leader who's qualified by experience.

Leadership requires us to be authentic. This means we have to be clear about our principles, our mission, and our intentions.

Big corporate companies refer to this as their mission statement or ethos.

And these are all qualities that lie within you already. It's your vision and how you want to influence others. And it's not something you can read or learn in a book, per se. Sure, you could get ideas and pointers. But we are all born with different leadership styles, which makes leadership an inside job! And it all starts with knowing yourself first.

When you know what you stand for, what you believe in, and where you're going, it becomes your blueprint.

It will help you have tough conversations, and it's the very thing that will help you know exactly who to bring on to your team and when it's time to let someone go.

When we stand in and operate from our values, we become the most authentic versions of ourselves and the best leaders we can be. It imparts a willingness to show up every day and be and do better than you did yesterday.

Becoming a leader of others starts with self-leadership. And self-leadership begins with acute self-awareness and the courage to stand up and speak out loud what you believe in.

I am a leader.

When I speak my truth, good things happen.

My authenticity turns me into an
influential leader.

I must lead myself before I can lead others.

Leadership is an inside job!

When I stand in and operate from my values,
I become an impactful leader.

1 *What do you believe in?*

2 *What is your personal mission and what are your goals?*

3 *What do you value/respect?*

4 *Who are some of your favorite leaders?*

- *What are their qualities that you admire?*

- *How can you weave them into your business?*

5 *What is your company's mission statement? What is the blueprint for values you want everyone to operate from?*

CHAPTER 14:

Achieving more while doing less

*"If we want to live a wholehearted life, we have to become
intentional about cultivating rest and play, and we must
work to let go of exhaustion as a status symbol and
productivity as self worth."*

– BRENÉ BROWN

C I remember listening to an interview with a multimillion-dollar coach. At the time, I was trying to do what so many business owners out there do as well. I was trying to find the magic bullet that would make me as successful as she was (and specifically, I was looking for the secret sauce that would do it overnight!).

As high-achieving individuals, we've all been mesmerized and bedazzled by other accomplished entrepreneurs' stories. We get obsessed with *how they* did it and their specific road map to affluence.

So we decide that we're going to do all the things that all the gurus say they did to attain their fortunes.

We hustle harder and faster, doing more and more and more.

Surely that is the best way to rapid success, right?

Wrong.

In our hurry from rags to riches, we break ourselves and our businesses.

You might be saying: "But Hanneke, you're the one who told us to make that commitment that we would do whatever it takes. Obviously, this is what has to be done?"

And my answer is yes, I did tell you to make this dedication to yourself. I did, however, also promise you more joy and ease in your business. And the road to that kind of blissful abundance isn't paved by someone else's blueprint to success.

Much like the singularity of our fingerprints, the path to our destiny has its own special code. And that code is locked up in your DNA.

Thus your job as a business owner should be one of constant self-discovery.

When you understand your personality traits and what makes you tick, it becomes easier for you to optimize your energy levels. And when we have more energy, we are able to go faster, smarter, and longer—without killing ourselves.

It is essential, then, that you learn how to work with instead of against yourself. Having this knowledge will allow you to create resiliency routines to overcome obstacles without the frustrating grind and resentment that plague so many entrepreneurs. Stay tuned: We'll cover more on that in Chapter 18.

For now, let's focus on unlocking your path of least resistance to your dreams.

To do so, I'm going to take you back to my late teens and early 20s. Before I learned about the power of implementing the Up Level Formula, I created a little coping mechanism to help me with my anxiety. Little did I know how severely that habit would backfire once it came to building a sustainable and profitable business.

Back then, my anxious spells would usually amplify when I was by myself and alone with my thoughts. I'd sit for hours doing absolutely nothing, trapped in my head while getting more and more distressed. I absolutely hated being in such a state. Not being able to sleep, feeling scared, and lonely all the time.

So I created a defense strategy: never be alone. Instead of learning how to process my feelings better, I decided I'd evade them by surrounding myself with people 24/7.

There were a few flaws in my fail-safe strategy. For starters, running away from myself wasn't exactly solving the core issue. It was just a Band-Aid.

And after discovering and implementing the principles of the Up Level Formula, I stopped running and started enjoying being in my own presence and in the present moment.

The second problem, and the one that brings us to the point of this chapter, is this: For most of my life, I operated and was perceived by everyone in my life as an extrovert.

I was very good at adapting, fitting in wherever you needed me to. I played into what I thought was expected of me. The "acting" became second nature.

And so I thought it was normal for an extrovert to:

- get sweaty palms and armpits when you walked into a room where you didn't know anyone.

- feel your heart trying to burst out of your chest when you were in conversation with someone else, and suddenly there was silence.

- take hours to unwind after a networking event.

- feeling exhausted all the time.

It turns out all of the above *was* normal.

They were normal for an INTROVERT.

That's correct. The Myers-Briggs personality type test revealed that yours truly was, in fact, an introvert, a discovery I made in my mid-30s while working with my business coach. Through our conversations, she had started to suspect that I was actually an introvert who had adapted to function as an extrovert.

She was right.

My mind was blown. How could I not have known this about myself?

Surrounding myself with people all the time not only made my anxiety worse, it added unnecessary pressure and left me extremely exhausted and drained.

I had designed my life to do the exact opposite of what I wanted. Everything in it was working against my natural rhythm and flow.

This revelation explained why I didn't cope well with and hated boarding school, and why my sales job left me depleted and frustrated.

It also explained why I would come home from eight or sometimes nine hours of teaching Pilates and just wanted to stare at the wall. When you're teaching for that many hours, it's very different from when you're in an office. There is no zoning out; you are on the entire time.

You're expending bucket loads of energy. And because I had no idea how to work with the cadence of who I really am at my core, I completely burnt myself and my Pilates business out.

When we understand the inner workings of our personality—how we work best, when we work best, what drains us, what fuels us—it becomes easier to manage our physical energy.

Unfortunately, most of us have no idea how to manage our energy levels properly. It also doesn't help that we've been brainwashed by mainstream society's belief that dictates that when we're not busy doing all.of.the.things.all.of.the.time, we are lazy and worthless.

Operating from this viewpoint left me spent and unable to achieve the success I desired.

But it is all good and worth it, right? I got to brag and wear my exhaustion as a badge of honor like it was some kind of status symbol that proved just how productive and worthy of success I was.

Wrong.

Listening to everyone else's stories, tips, and tricks on all the things I had to do to "get there" was basically the exact opposite of what I needed (and wanted) to attain prosperity.

Since making this discovery, I have taken many more personality tests, and when I start working with my clients, I have them take these tests too.

By combining all the information from these tests and paying closer attention to what fuels clients rather than what drains them, we are able to decipher their secret performance code, opening the gateway to achieving more while doing less.

Together we put words to what they are feeling, which gives them the language they need to express themselves and their needs better. This knowledge immediately improves their leadership and management skills.

We are also better able to:

- pinpoint where their blind spots are

- define their role in their business

- uncover the most effective management strategies

As a result, their businesses flourish. They are happier and experience way less guilt when they take time off to rest and play. And the best part is that their teams are happier, too.

Here's what one Up Level Program participant achieved after implementing and integrating the information of how she works best:

> The Up Level Program helped me take better care of my business by taking better care of myself, its leader. I learned how to work with my unique strengths and foster my own resiliency in order to be the most valuable asset possible for my business and team. This helped my 7-figure business stand up to the most challenging year it has ever faced.
>
> –ANDREA ISABELLE LUCAS, FOUNDER AND CEO OF BARRE & SOUL

After incorporating this knowledge into my life and how I operate, my anxiety went way down; I realized that I no longer identify as an anxious person. I have more energy. I get more done, and I work way less.

In the years since I started merging my personality traits into my life and working with my natural flow, my business became more profitable. My creativity increased, and my joy skyrocketed. (Oh, and I took more time off to do what I wanted when I wanted to do it—guilt-free—which meant more travel and family time!)

I live a more wholehearted life
when I include more rest and play.

The road to my success lights up
when I follow my blissful abundance.

When I work with my strengths and foster my
resiliency, I become my business'
most valuable asset.

When I implement the intricate workings
that make me unique into my life,
it unlocks a new dimension of what's
possible to achieve.

1 *Ever taken the Myers-Briggs personality test? Take it now. You can access a free version of the test by visiting 16personalities.com*

Bonus points: get your team to take it, too, and have a team meeting where everyone talks about what they learned about themselves, discuss their favorite strength and weakness.

2 *Other tests you can take and where to find them:*

- *How to Fascinate: howtofascinate.com*
- *Kolbe: secure.kolbe.com*
- *Human Design: jovianarchive.com/get_your_chart*

CHAPTER 15:

Have a little faith... in yourself

nother problem with looking to others to tell you you're doing a good job and always following others' advice is that you stop trusting yourself. In other words, you stop trusting what your intuition is trying to tell you.

Many of my private and Up Level Program clients come to me to become more confident as business owners. They are usually excellent at their craft but doubt themselves as leaders and business-savvy people.

They are sick of feeling like insecure imposters who are always relying on outside sources to tell them the right and wrong way to do something. They are ready to break out of the disempowering validation cycle that keeps them trapped in self-doubt.

This is exactly where I found myself a few years ago, right when I started my coaching business.

Although I had learned and applied so many of the steps we've already covered in this book, I still didn't trust myself. I was still very much looking for the approval of others and, as I mentioned before, I was still looking for that magic bullet that would instantly turn my business into an overnight success.

So, like most people, I was reading every single business book that I could lay my hands on. And as I mentioned in the previous chapter, I was listening to everyone and their mothers' advice on how I should run my business, what I should do, how I should do it.

You know that expression, "Too many cooks in the kitchen"? That was my business.

As a result, I was all over the place and more uncertain than ever about how to proceed. This way or that way—or their way?

It was at this very moment that I decided to make the biggest business investment I have ever made. I hired a business coach. Although I had worked with life and career coaches and had taken a whole bunch of business courses, I had never hired a coach to specifically focus on business growth.

In our sessions together, we uncovered, among lots of things, that I didn't trust myself. At all!

This obviously had to be fixed pronto. Here's how I did it.

- I practiced.

- I recommitted to myself (again!). It always starts with that self-commitment.

- I was going to work on my trust muscle every damn day until it was strong. Until I believed in myself and trusted myself, my abilities, and my gut 100%.

- Next, I knew I was going to need support. I was going to need someone to help me uncover my blind spots. That's where my business coach became invaluable. I had a built-in accountability partner who could call me out on my BS and kept me focused. (Truly, best investment ever!)

I treated this like I was training for a marathon.

Every single day for three or so months straight, I'd get up and listen to something inspirational and uplifting.

I meditated for 10 minutes every day. I monitored my language, my thoughts, my actions like a hawk. I worked and implemented all the components of the Up Level Formula like it was my job.

I wrote out mantras like these every day:

- I trust myself and the universe.

- Things always work out for me.

When I was making decisions, I would tune into how my body was feeling before I made a move. I started to notice what a "hell yes!" and a "nope" felt like in my body.

I tapped into which parts of my business were exciting to me and which were not. I also stopped listening to everyone and anyone's business tips. Instead, I picked a few people whom I really admired and trusted.

And slowly, my trust muscle became stronger.

A few months later, I remember sitting in one of my business mastermind meetings with my peers, and all of them wanted to know what the heck my secret was.

Over the course of three months, I had completely shifted my energy. For the first time in my life, I was calm and serene. Even my business coach was amazed by my transformation.

My confidence flourished as a result of the faith I had in myself and my business. All of a sudden, I instinctively knew what had to be done to grow it. The steps forward became more clear than ever before.

Even when things went wrong or didn't work out as planned, I was able to keep my cool, trusting that it's all working out for the greater good of everyone.

By harnessing this power, I completely transformed my business.

It helped me to stop looking for outside validation and permission from others so much.

Something else magically happened: I stopped comparing myself to others. I stayed in my lane. I accepted that I had my very own special mission to fulfill, that I was sent here for a different reason than anyone else. What everyone else was up to was none of my business.

Why let other people and their limiting opinions determine what's possible for you and your vision? We are all here to live out a very unique purpose! So another person's way is not your way. Stop letting them set the bar for you.

You are not here to be as successful as this or that business owner. And your trajectory isn't going to look or happen the same way as someone else's.

It reminds me of a quote from Tama Kieves' book "Inspired & Unstoppable: Wildly Succeeding in Your Life's Work!"

Kieves writes:

"We live in the Information Age, God help us, and we can start to believe in information, more than guidance. Somewhere along the way, we started trusting complete strangers on talk shows, Botoxed with serenity, more than our own instincts. That's got to stop.... Why listen to an 'expert' instead of a genius? ...

Sure, you can benefit from others. Just don't let it stop you from learning about your power. You already have a way to succeed…. It's embedded in the pockets of your ease."[26]

My trust gave me the creative freedom to finally run my business my own damn way versus the guru's way (or the way my so-called competitor was doing it). I became less fearful of doing something the right or wrong way, which opened the channel to so many possibilities that I hadn't considered. Letting go of the idea that there was a perfect way to do something allowed me to step into inspired action.

When you trust yourself and that everything always works out for the greater good of all, it becomes much easier to tap into and listen for intuitive nudges.

As one particular seven-figure business owner who I helped regain faith in herself and her abilities said, once she implemented our work, she was able to move through the fog and bring what's really valuable into focus. Accessing her intuition helped her raise money with more confidence.

Your gut is a direct download from your inner wisdom. Our intuition is the most powerful tool we have. As the dictionary's meaning of intuition explains: "It's something you understand immediately, without conscious reasoning."

When you trust yourself, you no longer feel the need to explain or justify your decisions because you know that you're acting on your truth.

And it's important that you not only start to flex your trust muscle, but also acknowledge what this knowing feels like in your body. It's different for all of us. For me, personally, it's an expansive sensation, something that I feel I'm being pulled toward.

When you can connect with that fountain of trust and infinite wisdom that lies inside you, magic happens. You're able to overcome all the setbacks; you're able to get up when you stumble, brush yourself off, and try again. And you're able to figure out the best path forward much faster.

And the first step to building this trust is always cultivating awareness.

Why do you feel uncertain? What is the reason for seeking that outside validation or permission? Or asking others what you should do?

Using the Up Level Formula to understand where this behavior comes from makes it easier to deconstruct and release it, and other times it's enough to simply know that it's there.

From there, it's all about being diligent and consistently training your trust muscle to become stronger.

Your blueprint to success is already here; all you need to do is learn how to tune into the infinite wisdom that's locked up inside you.

When I make a bet on myself, by investing in the support I need, it always pays off.

I trust that things are always working out for the greater good of all, even when it doesn't look like it now.

When I trust myself, I stop looking for outside validation and permission from others.

I already have a way to succeed. It's embedded within me.

Faith in myself gives me creative freedom to do what I want, when I want.

When I let go of perfection, I allow myself to step into the realm of inspired possibilities.

I stay in my lane—other people's business is none of my mine.

My gut is a direct download from my inner wisdom.

My intuition is the most powerful tool I have.

1 *Listen to something inspiring first thing in the morning.*

2 *Write out a mantra that will help you trust yourself and the universe. For me, it was exactly that: "I trust myself and the universe. Things are always working out for me."*

3 *Meditate:*
Access your bonus guided clarity meditation that I've recorded for you on the book resources page by visiting: hannekeantonelli.com/book-bonus

On the Rise

CHAPTER 16:

The beautiful but bumpy road to integration

"Change is hard at first, messy in the middle, and gorgeous at the end."

–ROBIN SHARMA

Like most people right out of college, it took me a while to find my footing. Up until then, there had been a lot of structure from boarding school, ballet, music, and then a full college workload with a couple of side-hustle jobs. For most of my life, I didn't really have any extra time in my schedule.

Then I decided to move to England, a country I had never visited before and where I knew only a handful of people, including one of my brothers. Back then, it was very popular for South Africans to take advantage of their two-year working holiday visa, which was one of the perks of being part of the British Commonwealth. I had just finished university with a big student loan that needed to be paid down pronto.

Unlike in the U.S., students borrow money from banks in South Africa at normal interest rates. And back in 2004, I had a loan with a 7% interest rate. So moving to London was a good way to travel a little bit while also working in a more robust economy and currency and ultimately paying down my loan faster. I was able to do the latter in less than three years.

Moving to England was a massive uplevel for a farm girl from rural South Africa. And landing my first job in the accounts department of a Japanese travel company posed an extremely steep learning curve. Fun fact: I was fired from this job because, in the words of my boss, "It's sad to see someone with such high intellect and so little people skills." Guess what my next job was? A broker in London's financial markets where it was all about having interpersonal skills. See? Never allow other people and their misguided opinions to define you and your potential.

That said, I'm not surprised by my boss' observation. In a little under three months, I had completely uprooted my life. I was in a new, very polite culture, and my "call a spade a spade" South African directness was quite often misinterpreted as rude. It also definitely didn't help that my English, although very good, was still not at its best, which made expressing myself a little difficult every now and then. That, of course, led to more incidents of being perceived as blunt.

Something else that was completely foreign to me was figuring out how to safely navigate a public transport system, something that I'd never had to do before.

I also hadn't yet developed a strong social structure or grounding routine, both of which took me years to establish. As a result, I was skittish, homesick, anxious, and, thus, probably a little irritable at work. The term millennial wasn't yet a thing, but I probably exuded all of the annoying work habits of my generation. I still had a limited understanding of workplace etiquette and was a very entitled and naive 22-year-old.

Those first few months in London were some of the toughest ones ever. It gave being lonely a whole new meaning, feeling completely out of my league and overwhelmed by all of it. I was so far outside of my comfort zone.

By now, you've probably realized that while building your business, there will be plenty of times where you'll experience these out-of-your-depth feelings as well. And you may very well be feeling those emotions now that you've started to implement some of the tools I've provided in this book. You've taken some huge leaps, and it's natural to feel overwhelmed and unsettled right now.

When first adopting all the strategies I've shared, you will experience a big learning curve. You'll also start to see a few exciting results. Some of these may be massive shifts that happen so quickly that it may take you a second to catch up to the impact it's having on you and your business.

And in this catching-up phase, it's important to remember that it's completely normal for you to have all the feelings. You're in a period of integration where your mind is still busy processing all of the changes.

It's extremely important that you stop holding yourself to perfection and allow the road to be what it is: bumpy.

During this stage of the Up Level Program, my companion online-course for this book, clients will often swing between feeling extremely excited about the future and also a little unsure of how to proceed.

By implementing the Up Level Formula, they've already cultivated the awareness to know what behaviors don't lead to the results they want. But they haven't yet developed new habits that they can trust to accomplish their goals. During this stage, it's critical to realize that uncertainty is merely that, and uneasy feelings don't mean they're doing something wrong.

It's here where lots of self-judgment and impatience can come into play. When we judge and beat ourselves up, we slow down the integration of new sustainable growth. Accepting our humanness and practicing self-compassion will help us to go further faster.

That's why it's so important for you to be aware and identify when you're in a period of integration in your business. And yes, it usually comes once you've made a leap and achieved a big goal.

Let's take a minute to explain what I mean by integration. According to the Merriam-Webster dictionary, to integrate is "to form, coordinate, or blend into a functioning or unified whole."

The path to full integration comes through love and self-acceptance.

Much like when I was still learning to use London's Underground in the most efficient way, and learning which buses and trains would get me to where I needed to go fastest, you're currently learning a whole new way of operating.

In the beginning, I'd get on a train going in the wrong direction or would take a circuitous route, which meant I'd show up late or not at all. Sure, it was frustrating and nerve-wracking, but then after a while, it became second nature. My brain absorbed the information, and I no longer felt scared of taking trains and buses.

In fact, it became such a part of me that I remember being quite sad my last weekend living in London and riding a bus route that saved so much time. Soon, I'd be moving to New York City and learning a different transport system.

My learning curve will be similar to how you'll experience the journey of integration. You'll eventually reach a new destination in your business where you'll have to adapt and go through the integration phase yet again.

Part of the integration period requires some reflection and active thinking about the process you're undergoing, and the other part requires you not to think about it at all. It requires you to just be: go for walks, sleep enough, do something fun and creative. Did someone say get a hobby?

The sooner you as an entrepreneur realize that building a business has less to do with the end result and everything to do with creating a fun journey, the more joy, growth, and ease you'll experience.

So how does one get more delight out of the wild ride of business ownership and integrate all your newfound knowledge?

I usually start by having my clients reflect on their journey.

We look at all the lessons they've learned, how far they've come, what they've accomplished.

And then, we look for patterns and credibility markers of past experiences that led to success. These serve as their new road map to action.

Having these "success maps" in your back pocket will allow you to stay confident and trust your ability to achieve a specific goal. This is when it's crucial to remain patient, let go of the outcome, and stop judging yourself and the process. Allow for all the new habits to become your new gorgeous normal and accept that it may get a little messy at times.

When I try doing something in a new way,
it's normal to have all the feelings.

I release self-judgment and impatience;
I choose self-compassion.

I practice grace and humility and
accept my humanness.

My path to full integration comes through love
and self-acceptance.

The more I focus on having fun on the journey
to my goal, the easier it is to attain success.

1 *Think of some big goals you achieved in business: How did you feel a few days or weeks after achieving that goal?*

2 *What lessons did you learn on your way to accomplishing the goal?*

3 *How did you know you had integrated these lessons and made them your new normal?*

4 *Look for patterns: What are some actions/thoughts that consistently surfaced and helped you achieve that goal?*

CHAPTER 17:

Speed up the upleveling process by stepping into the future

A few years ago, I went on a business retreat. One of my peers whom I had been in a mastermind program with the year before was there too. The last time we had been in contact, she had completely dismantled her business and was starting from scratch.

At the time, she was showing up to our calls frustrated that rebuilding her business was taking so much work and so long. On one of those calls, I pointed out that her language was out of alignment with attaining her goals faster. She was constantly using words that suggested that things would take longer and that everything would be hard. She messaged me after the call to thank me for that insight and told me that my observation had a profound impact on her.

My time in the mastermind drew to a close a little while after that, and we lost touch. As soon as I saw her at the retreat, I could feel a difference in her presence; something monumental had happened.

And then, during one of our group sessions, I learned what it was. In the year since talking with her, she'd taken her business from $0 in revenue to $250,000, and the physical year wasn't done yet. She was most likely going to close out the year at $300,000.

When asked what she had done differently, she said: "I woke up every day and asked myself, if I already ran a six-figure business, how would I act? What would I be saying? What would I have to believe? How would I be using my time?"

By incorporating this same tactic in my coaching process with clients, I've helped them to speed up attaining their results.

And here's how and why it works so well.

In our journey throughout this book, you've gained clarity on your vision, and you've used the Up Level Formula to align your actions with the results you want.

And as we discovered in the previous chapter, when we make all these new adjustments, things can feel very unfamiliar and messy. All too often, this change becomes overwhelming, and that can cause clients to shut down or revert back to old patterns that no longer serve them.

So what does it take to allow yourself to stay in the room, stay committed, and make that future vision your reality now?

To get to that answer, I want to take you back to when I was a little girl.

You know how some girls dream about getting married and know exactly how many children they want? Yeah, that wasn't me. I never thought that far into the future. There was only one time that I can remember when an ex-boyfriend and I imagined what it would be like to have a baby.

We were driving in his truck—or a Bakkie as we refer to it in South Africa (pronounced "buck-key")—back from a weekend getaway with friends. I was cuddled up right next to him as we were driving, warm and safe, and dreaming of our future with kids.

It was all very cute and puppy-love romantic at the time, especially considering we were both still virgins. I was 18 and finishing up my final year of high school. He was to inherit his parents' farm, and I had my eye on a big finance job after finishing up uni. Needless to say, we broke up as soon as I hit college.

Then there was a time before my husband and I were married that we briefly discussed what religion we would raise our kids. Funnily enough, our wedding song ended up being "You & Me" by Dave Matthews Band, and one of the lines in the chorus is "and when the kids are old enough, we're gonna teach them to fly."

And since then, we've always been on a "in five years we'll try" plan, so I think you're catching my drift: I'm still not sure that I see children in my future.

Contrast that with so many of the girls I went to high school with and even my sister-in-law. They knew to their core, without a doubt, that they wanted to be moms, raising families, with the idyllic picket-fence life.

I remember the night that my sister-in-law, who had been dreaming about having babies and being a mom since she was, like, 16, told us that they were going to start trying. She also confessed that she was all of a sudden not sure and nervous and having all the feelings.

She was 24 at the time, and I remember my inside voice going: "Um, you know you can wait, right? You're still so young. You have a whole lifetime to do this. Go travel, see the world!" But those were my values, and having just met her a few months earlier, it was most definitely not my place to voice this opinion.

What I didn't yet understand was this: My sister-in-law was clear and confident about what she wanted her future to be. However, just because she was sure about what she wanted didn't mean she wasn't also scared. She was about to take a massive leap of faith and create the future that she'd always dreamt of. Being anxious about that leap was natural.

A few months later, my sister-in-law was pregnant—and flourished as a mom!

We often think that if we have fear around our goals and ambitions, then they must be wrong. And so we wait and wait and wait and think and think and think to see if we can come up with a better, more "perfect" vision that doesn't scare us.

But my sister-in-law knew the truth: the more significant our dreams and the clearer we are about them, the more likely they are to instill some fear in us.

Why?

Because a lot of us are afraid of getting exactly what we want. Deep down, most of us are afraid of success and haunted by questions like:

What if I don't like it?
What if it's too much to handle?
What if I'm too busy and burn myself out?
What if...

And by doing this, we delay realizing our dreams.

It's here where my clients benefit greatly from the exercise of embodying who they imagine they'll be in the future.

Going back to my sister-in-law, what she essentially did so graciously when she announced that they were going to start trying for kids was this: she stepped into her future self.

She became the person she wanted to be, namely a mom at that very moment. She called her future dream toward her, and she embodied it. Actually, come to think of it, she had been embodying that vision since she was a little girl who'd run around the house with a pillow stuffed under her shirt, pretending she was pregnant.

She kept her eye trained on her vision and then eventually realized it. And my business friend mentioned above did exactly the same thing to get her from a failing business to $250,000 in revenue in under a year. A beautiful example of upleveling right there.

The other benefit that happens by incorporating more of your future self's qualities now, is that it strips the notion that you have to completely reinvent yourself and become someone else to accomplish your dreams.

That's another bogus lie. You are already that successful, amazingly talented person you want to become. The only thing standing in your way are the habits not in alignment with the success you want, and the Up Level Formula is your gateway to breaking those pesky patterns.

So what is your vision? And more specifically, how do you feel and act in that future vision?

"It's not really about what you achieve. It's about who you become as a consequence of the chase." Those are wise words from Dr. Jim Loehr [27], author and performance psychologist.

And I couldn't agree more.

The reason we set goals and our driving force behind them has way more to do with the feeling we believe we'll experience when we attain that objective.

So what are the feelings you're chasing?
Who do you want to become?
What does that version of you say, believe, and do?
Let's go even more granular when you think of your future self:
Are you happy with where you live?
What car do you drive?
Where do you travel to?
What qualities do you exude every day?

Sometimes an easier way to access that vision is to revisit an exercise we explored earlier in this book. Fill in the blanks:

One day when _____ happens, then I will _____.

What are those missing parts for you?

Is it: One day, when my business brings in a million dollars, then I'll go on vacation? Or perhaps it means you'll buy that expensive bag or get a massage?

Or is it: One day, when my business makes eight figures, then I'll finally feel calm?

Just like my sister-in-law, to summon your future vision, you have to embody parts of it now.

So if you never take a vacation, book a trip.
Get the massage. Buy the bag. Now, not later.

You can even dig deeper and think of what qualities you portray in that future version of yourself:

Are you more centered, more patient? Are you bolder, do you speak your mind more?
How can you start to embody parts of that future version of yourself in this very moment?

Embodying and incorporating as much of your future desires now also has the following benefits:

1. It makes the journey to your goal easier and more fun.
   Often as business owners, we have a tendency to punish ourselves. Because we are such driven people, we're hard and demanding on ourselves, not allowing simple little treats like a spa day or a day of complete rest. We, of course, already know that this has a lot to do with the conditioning of a sick world that tells us that it's wrong, bad, and lazy to chill out and makes us feel guilty for having fun.

   But, as we discovered earlier in this book, when you're constantly depriving yourself of the little joys in life, you won't be able to go as far or be as successful as you want to be. When you incorporate some of these simple pleasures into your daily routine, then you're happier. And that will make you more resilient.

2. Incremental upgrades help support exponential growth.
   In Chapter 9, we discussed sabotaging behaviors that happen as a result of the subconscious mind trying to keep us safe and avoid something we perceive as wrong. We saw that this often happens

right after you have a massive breakthrough or win in your business or life. This undermining tendency will pull you right back into that less amazing version of yourself, slowing down your ability to create success.

When we practice embodying our future self every day, we make incremental upgrades to our patterns and behaviors. These subtle upgrades build momentum that leads to great success that seemingly happens overnight.

I already possess all the qualities to make my
dreams a reality; I deploy those traits now.

By rewarding myself often,
I experience more joy.

The more fun I have, the easier it is to
accomplish my goals.

Investing in incremental upgrades supports
my exponential growth.

Embodying my future successful self now
accelerates my journey to success.

UP LEVEL
IT NOW:

1 *What is the future vision you have? What is the goal you want to attain?*

2 *Imagine you've already achieved that objective:*

- *What qualities do people who hit that goal already exude?*
- *How do they act? What do they say/believe/think?*
- *How does your future self tackle specific challenges?*

3 *How can you start to embody some of the above today? Remember, it's ok to start small and then make incremental upgrades to incorporate and embody more of that future version of you daily.*

CHAPTER 18:

The little things that boost big results

I f there's one thing I know about entrepreneurs, it's this: We are resilient AF. And the more we can train our resiliency muscles, the better!

When we are able to harness our ability to be adaptable to whatever life throws our way, the impossible becomes possible. We make better decisions. We see opportunities faster. We lead better, and we become victorious.

So how does one do this?

It all comes down to your sustainable success habits. Some people call it a resiliency routine, others a sacred list. Whatever you want to call it, the basic principle to remember is this:

You are your business' biggest asset. Without you, there is no business. So in order for your business to thrive, you have to be in tip-top shape mentally and physically.

Think of it as the safety instructions on an airplane. They are always telling us to put our oxygen masks on first before we help others.

The same applies to entrepreneurs. For you to be able to take care of your clients, your staff, and all the other things that go into running a booming business, you have to be thriving. This principle applies to everyone who's in a leadership role, whether that's a school principal, a parent, a CEO, or a manager.

If you start to put your business and others' needs before your own, which all entrepreneurs do at some point, you and your business (and everyone who depends on you) will suffer in the long run.

That's why it's crucial to incorporate habits that will support your mental and physical health into your daily routine. Again, this is something that most entrepreneurs say they will do in the future. But putting this off will most definitely lead to burnout and health problems, and you'll run your business into the ground. Remember me and my Pilates business? I completely didn't have a resiliency routine back then.

As one Up Level Program member said, it's usually the topics that they resist and avoid that give them the best growth opportunities. So if you're feeling a little resistance to this one, take it as your cue to lean into this chapter. Trust me; you'll come out better and stronger on the other side.

Your resiliency routine is also extremely important to help you nail your results. It upgrades everything in our Up Level Formula:

Beliefs + Thoughts + Language + Feelings + Actions = **Results**

More specifically, having your resiliency routine will help you to feel good on a cellular level, which is the opposite of what stress will do to your body and mind. Although our bodies are built to sustain small doses of stress, they are not equipped to cope with persistent periods of duress.

Long-term stress can and will have devastating effects on your life, including your mental and physical health. But when you have a routine with sustainable success habits designed to relieve stress, you'll thrive in the most challenging of times.

It's also important to remember that everyone's resiliency list will look different. We all have different personalities and interests. Extroverts will probably have "drinks with a friend" on their list, while introverts may have "stay in and read a book" on theirs.

This list is your list. It can contain anything and everything that makes you feel calm, fulfilled, and happy.

When constructing your resiliency routine, think about things that you can do daily, weekly, and monthly that will allow you to feel nurtured and fulfilled. The idea here is not to add more stuff to your already-crammed to-do list; instead, view this routine as a way to create some space for yourself.

When you have a resiliency routine, little things become an essential part of your daily life: meditating, making yourself a beautiful cup of tea, and enjoying it quietly on your favorite couch or your favorite cafe for five minutes.

Which brings us to the next point: Your daily resiliency routine isn't a one-and-done thing. That's why I called it a routine. It becomes habitual, like brushing your teeth is something you'll never skip. You do it no matter what, and it doesn't have to be a drawn-out process. Small moments of embracing and appreciating what brings you joy will go a long way. And those moments can and often will evolve. My personal resiliency routine shifts and changes with the seasons.

Once you've established your routine, you'll have to put firm boundaries around it.

When I was little, we were never allowed into my parents' bedroom without knocking first, and yet I always wanted to barge in and jump into bed with my mom like I saw my friends do when sleeping over at their house. Instead, I remember standing in front of the big dark mahogany door after knocking, waiting for my mother's "yes, come in" and then walking into the room to find her perched on my dad's side of the bed, reading a magazine, almost as if she were hiding something from me.

When I asked my mom about this years later, she explained why they had this firm boundary: "We had three kids. Our room was my safe and quiet retreat, a space where your dad and I could escape the madness and take some time for ourselves."

Without knowing it, my mom and dad had established their own resiliency routine. Today, of course, I'm grateful for the lesson about boundaries.

So how can you create a sanctuary in your own life?

Here's what my daily resiliency routine looks like at the moment:

- Read something that inspires me, like my favorite quotes or nuggets of wisdom from my favorite author

- Meditate for 10-20 minutes

- Write for an hour (this was my routine while writing this book, which is why I was able to do the first draft in under 90 days)

- Do 30 minutes of exercise

- Have my morning coffee with my husband while he tells me about the news

A few important things to note:

I don't always get to everything on this list, nor do I do it in the same order or at the same time every day, and I don't beat myself up if I skip something.

The whole idea here is that you do something daily that makes you feel satisfied, calm, inspired, or successful. What is the feeling that you most desire to feel? What can you do daily or weekly that conjures that feeling in you? This further builds on the concept we discussed in the previous chapter of embodying your future self now.

To establish a routine like this, you'll first have to get clear on the things that light you up, and then you'll have to make those actions a priority. And finally, much like my parents, you'll have to make these habits sacred and enforce firm boundaries around them.

We—not anyone else—decide what our priorities are. And as a business owner, your well-being must always be your top priority. No exceptions. You have to start thinking of yourself as an athlete who's always in training. Building a business is a marathon. How fit are you right now?

I am my business' biggest asset and
treat myself as such.

Having my sustainable success habits
helps me thrive in challenging times.

I always make my resiliency routine
a top priority.

Growing my business is like running a
marathon; I always ensure I'm in tip-top shape.

1 *What activities do you love? Think about creative projects, hobbies, exercise, social interactions.*

- *What lights you up? Examples: museums, travel, gardening, hiking, reading, journaling, meditation, etc.*

- *Separate these activities into something you can do daily and things you'll incorporate weekly, monthly, or quarterly.*

- *Remember to schedule these activities on your calendar, because otherwise, they won't happen, and you'll keep pushing them off. When you allow yourself these simple pleasures, you'll not only feel happier, but you'll also come up with so many more creative ideas that will enable your business to have an even more significant impact on the world.*

2 *Looking for a daily practice that will help you become more strategic and focused? Get my bonus Up Level Daily Practice from the book resources page here: hannekeantonelli.com/book-bonus*

CHAPTER 19

From lacking it all to having it all

The illusion of scarcity is nothing new. Civilization has always operated from the mindset of lacking something. We've fought wars that have prompted whole countries to hoard resources. This mentality is fueled by fear. When we act from this place, the human race becomes a disgrace. We become our worst selves.

Most business owners experience this scarcity mindset around money. No matter how big their business, there is always a worry about where the money will come from next, if there will be enough, and if they will be able to make more. And, of course, this all makes a lot of sense because no money equals no business.

As author Richard Dotts points out in his book "Dollars Flow to Me Easily," financial freedom has become the ultimate goal of modern society.[28] I know that that's definitely a huge part of why I started my business, and it's the same for almost all my clients too. We all want to create a company that will allow us to do what we want, when we want to do it.

We've also been conditioned to expect that money brings happiness. And when we have money, our lives are perfect.

But as Denise Duffield-Thomas notes in her book "Get Rich, Lucky Bitch!: Release Your Money Blocks and Live a First-Class Life,"[29] if money brings happiness, then why do we have so many wealthy celebrities who suffer from depression or get divorced?

Money is one of the most loaded topics, and we have all sorts of beliefs, feelings, and thoughts about it. Most of them are negative, which makes talking about it a nightmare for many business owners.

It's no wonder that they ignore the topic completely—not knowing their numbers and unable to sell their services and products without feeling nervous and weird about it.

Which brings us to one of my other favorite quotes by author Jen Sincero. In her book "You Are a Badass at Making Money: Master the Mindset of Wealth," she writes: "When it comes to having sex and making money, you're supposed to know what you're doing and be all great at it, but nobody teaches you anything about it, and you're never supposed to talk about it because it's inappropriate, dirty, not so classy."[30]

In short: most of us have some money baggage. And when you bring that baggage into your business (or any relationship, for that matter), it can cause major drama and stress.

Your beliefs about money will directly affect how much you make, how much you pay your staff, and a whole lot more.

The relationship that we have with our money reminds me of toilet paper in boarding school.

We used to refer to it as white gold. Instead of stocking the bathrooms with toilet paper, the boarding school I attended in South Africa realized that people were wasting TP when they had it at the ready in the bathrooms. Like all kids, boarding-school teenagers love to do silly things with toilet paper. So to save on costs, every student would get only one roll of toilet paper every two weeks. (Or perhaps it was one per week? I can't remember now, but toilet paper was scarce!)

As a result, there were two scenarios that you absolutely never wanted to find yourself in:

1. Losing your toilet paper or running out of it—hence you locked your TP up in your dorm room closet.

2. Finding yourself in desperate need to use the restroom when you were nowhere near your precious toilet paper.

And unfortunately, one afternoon, I found myself in both these pickles.

First, I was what felt like miles away from my room and already dying to use the bathroom. It also didn't help that I was in a hurry to get to a ballet session. So in an effort to kill two birds with one stone, when I finally entered my room, I quickly stripped down to my birthday suit and grabbed my leotard, thinking I'd get dressed while going to the loo.

But then disaster No. 2 struck: my toilet paper wasn't in its usual place. I couldn't hold it any longer, so I decided "screw it" and made a beeline for the bathroom, butt naked, where I happened to run into my roommate. She took one look at me and started dying laughing while waving the most treasured commodity, saying: "Want the toilet paper? Come and get it."

It's right here where I completely lost it and started giggling uncontrollably (like only a high-school girl can) and tinkling myself just a wee bit before I finally got to my desired destination of relief, laced with a tinge of embarrassment. Needless to say, I never misplaced my TP after that day.

Much like we viewed toilet paper in high school (and again at the beginning of the COVID-19 pandemic, right?), we also view wealth as a rare and limited commodity that takes a lot of hustle to achieve.

We are in a rush to make that money fast, out of fear that we'll miss our only opportunity to get rich. And, of course, this creates the illusion of more scarcity and extra emotional drama around money.

So how do you heal your relationship with money?

The answer lies in the Up Level Formula and using it to specifically look at your beliefs, thoughts, language, feelings, and actions around wealth.

Beliefs + Thoughts + Language + Feelings + Actions = **Results**

By implementing this process, you'll be able to see what is out of alignment with your money goals and make the necessary adjustments to earn more with ease.

From there, we can untangle ourselves from the illusion that money will solve all of our problems and bring us happiness. We realize that experiencing abundance is a state of mind, and the more we can harness that feeling, the easier it becomes to make money and experience joy.

This further builds on the concept of upleveling and speeding up the process that we discussed in Chapter 17. When we can summon that state of abundance now instead of in the future, it unlocks a whole new world of happiness and well-being in this very moment.

It also sets us free from the habit of hustling harder and depriving ourselves of all the joyful things that enrich our lives.

Here's how it played out for me:

While on Wall Street, I shifted my focus from all the many blessings I had, like a beautiful apartment and enough money to travel and buy almost anything my little heart desired. Instead, I homed in on the lack of romance. As a result of emphasizing that one area where there wasn't abundance, I deprived myself of enjoying the other parts that were plentiful.

And it didn't stop there.

When I started my Pilates business, love was abundant. But then my focus strayed to not having enough money. So I started working harder and harder, and, no matter how much money I made, it didn't feel like it was enough. Why?

Because I worked myself to the bone and completely neglected my other relationships, work became the only thing that held my attention.

I see many business owners do this same thing.

In pursuit of achieving financial and time flexibility, they often create prison-like circumstances instead. A few years into their business, they find themselves utterly deprived, overworked, and miserable.

Entrepreneurs get so fixated on their business results that they discard all their other achievements and many beautiful things in their lives. And this, of course, is such a dangerous loop to get stuck in because when you never stop to look back and give yourself credit for how far you've come or observe all that is going well, you'll always be hungry for more. And more will never be enough. Eventually, in your quest for more, you'll crash and burn, losing everything else that you once enjoyed.

We are multidimensional beings, with many aspects that make us feel alive. We were not built to focus on just one thing to make us feel satisfied and successful.

When we shift our focus to the bigger picture, we also release our death grip on our goals. Essentially, this helps us to shed our rigid expectations and control over how we think things must happen and thereby become more receptive to even better outcomes. Viewing life through a wider lens makes us more open to ideas we might have missed when we were so stuck in our old mode of thinking.

Something that greatly helped me to broaden my perspective is gratitude. Being thankful was a big thing that was missing from my life for a long time. Yes, gratitude is quite the trend in the personal-development world right now, and for good reason: it works. By putting gratitude in my attitude, I was finally able to feel whole on a level that was previously impossible for me.

I even got my hubby involved. Every night we name three things that we're grateful for that happened in our day. It's become a fun little ritual that we do together. Sometimes it's simple things like the ice cream we ate; other times, it's big stuff like signing new clients.

Focusing on all the fantastic things that don't have anything to do with your business will expand your vision of success and inspire you to acknowledge the outstanding work you achieve every day.

When you heal your relationship with money, practice gratitude, and learn how to embrace those abundant feelings now, your life becomes fuller, richer, and you'll feel happier and more alive. And this will have a ripple effect that spreads to your business.

This will empower you to spot opportunities, innovate, and add revenue streams more easily and faster.

It's this very process that helped one of our Up Level Program members to land the biggest client project of their career (in the middle of the pandemic, no less). By incorporating these steps, along with some of the other ones mentioned in this book, they not only saw a new opportunity, but had fun working toward it and earned almost $200,000 in additional income.

When I act from fear, I become
incredibly ineffective.

I create a company that allows me
the freedom to do what I want,
when I want to do it.

Experiencing abundance is a state of mind.

I am a multidimensional being,
with many aspects that make me feel alive.

By viewing life through a wider lens, I see
possibilities and experience abundance.

Practicing gratitude instantly shifts me into a
state of satisfaction, peace, and success.

UP LEVEL IT NOW:

1 *Gain insight into your relationship with money by using the Up Level Formula:*

Beliefs + Thoughts + Language + Feelings + Actions = **Results**

What are those concerning money and how you earn it?

How do they influence your actions?

What needs to be adjusted?

2 *Stepping into abundance: How rich and abundant does your life feel right now?*

Rate the following areas on a scale of 1-10 (with "1" being not at all, "10" being very):

- *Fun & recreation*
- *Physical environment*
- *Career*
- *Money*
- *Health*
- *Friends & family*
- *Romance/Significant other*
- *Personal growth*

What areas are feeling super neglected?

What areas feel great?

Pick two or three areas that you'd like to work on.

What is one thing you can do in each area that will improve your feelings of abundance? (Incremental upgrades go a long way!)

3 Celebrating and acknowledging your wins:

Looking at the categories in No. 2, write out a few small wins/good things that have happened in each category.

4 Practicing gratitude:

Start a daily practice of acknowledging three things you're grateful for. Remember: they can be big or small things and bonus points if you get your significant other to participate too.

CHAPTER 20:

Hello, success—and freedom!

While living in London in 2007, a friend and I decided to do a girl's trip to Portugal over the Easter weekend. This was also the same weekend that my life coach had given me the assignment to write down what I wanted in a significant other. And she gave me another exercise similar to the one you got in the previous chapter.

Once we arrived in Portugal in the afternoon, my girlfriend and I were wiped. We had gotten up at 3 a.m. that morning to get to the airport, so she decided to take a nap.

I opted to take a walk along the beach instead. I had never visited anywhere where English wasn't heard all around. I stepped into a corner store to get a magazine, but to my surprise, all of them were in Portuguese. (Duh.)

So I walked past the boardwalk and onto the beach with my journal and started "working" on my two assignments. The first one was about how I wanted to divvy up my time among family, friends, work, career, travel, health, and self-development.

Here was my drawing.

And then I wrote down my list of what I wanted in a man. Here it is:

"Wat ek soek" means "What I'm looking for":

Fun/good humor
Loving
Giving
Caring/compassionate
Willing to explore
Strong
Ambitious
Same morals and values
Respectful

WAT EK SOEK:
- fun / gd humour
- loving
- giving
- caring / compassionate
- willing to explore
- strong.
- Ambitious
- Morally same / value.
- Respectful.

An hour or so later, I was done with the exercises, and my friend was still napping in our hotel room. I was enjoying the springtime sun on my face, the sound of the ocean, and the sand under my feet. But there was also something else I started to notice.

Laughter and fun.

Not far from where I was sitting, there was a group of Americans in their 20s, three guys and a girl, who were having a ball. These friends were playing in the sand and occasionally had people from different countries stop by their group. This made it even more intriguing. Who were they? What were they doing here in Portugal? And how did they know so many people from around the world?

Up to that point, the only thing I knew about Americans was that they were loud, could be perceived to be a little obnoxious, and had the biggest economy in the world.

And here they were—definitely loud but fun, in an endearing way that made you feel happy just watching them. As the minutes ticked by, I became more and more drawn to them. Like a moth to a flame, I was mesmerized by their spontaneous laughter, something I wasn't getting enough of at age 25.

And then something else happened. I got a little nervous that they were going to leave and that my friend and I wouldn't have gotten a chance to meet them. That stung. I couldn't *not* meet this intriguing group!

Having now been on the beach for a few hours, I realized that these people were our gateway to an extremely fun weekend. So I rang my girlfriend up and told her to come join me on the beach to make friends with the American crew.

Caroline, who's Scottish and more introverted than I am, was a little reluctant, and I remember her asking if they were cute. At that very moment, my eyes were fixated on the tall, dark one with the incredibly sexy legs, and I told her, "Yeah, kinda." Yes, I was being coy.

It felt like forever before Caroline got down to the beach, and I started to have an increasingly panicked feeling that the group would leave and we'd never be able to meet them. She finally arrived, and I walked over somewhat awkwardly to introduce myself.

"Hi, guys. Would you mind if me and my girlfriend came over and sat with you? She's had a bit of a rough day," I said, fibbing to meet them. "We've noticed that you're the only people on the beach who speak English, too."

And so we met. There was the couple, Scott and Lauren. Mike, the poi spinner (more commonly known as a fire spinner), who was the reason everyone had gathered in Portugal. He had landed a contract with a Cirque du Soleil-type show that was running at a local casino for 10 months.

Mike had studied political science and was clued in on South African politics, so he peppered me with questions.

But I kept glancing at the one with the great smile who caught my eye with his Adrien Brody look. What was his story? His name was Bob, and it turned out that he was a musician and taught theater to kids.

Caroline and I ended up spending most of our time with this group, and we had the most fun that we had had in a very long time. After the weekend, I invited Scott, Lauren, and Bobby, who was lighthearted and charming and loved whiskey as much as I did—and whom I now had a massive crush on—to come visit me in London. I lived smack in the center of the city next to London Bridge, so they'd be able to get around and see all the sights easily if they stayed with me.

I had never laughed that much or slept so little over the course of seven days.

Back then, I was pretty uptight, maybe even a snob. Tainted by banking culture and operating from the belief that money equals happiness (and superiority), I looked down on those who didn't earn as much as I did. How could anyone possibly be happy if they didn't make lots of money? I'm not proud of who I was and how I thought about the world, but there it was.

So this American group totally threw me for a loop. A poi spinner and two musicians? The girl in the bunch at least had a respectable job, I thought to myself. How could they possibly be content?

The joke was on me. Their happiness was infectious. I had never seen anyone have so much freaking fun, be so spontaneous, and go with the flow.

I figured maybe it was just because we had all been on vacation together. But over the next few months, I got to know Bobby, and he totally stole my heart with his charismatic, caring, and sincere nature. This guy enjoyed dancing and music as much as I did, and he could make me laugh and laugh and then laugh some more.

He got along with and charmed all my friends, and I came to realize that there was nothing fake about him. He exuded the first quality that I was looking for in a man: fun. But he didn't just portray the first trait on my list of what I wanted in a partner; he embodied them all!

Three months into our long-distance relationship from London to Boston, I knew that he was the one I was going to marry.

Bob's happiness and the qualities he brought out in me became a drug. He had woken up the parts of myself that I had forgotten. Suddenly, my creative juices and can-do attitude that got me to Wall Street in the first place were flowing again.

Slowly, I started to realize that the way I was looking at the world was a bit topsy-turvy. Money doesn't equal happiness, after all. And my definition of success was also out of whack.

As I studied my lover over the months to come, I started to notice what made him so darn happy. He was living a life according to what *he* wanted.

When you live life by your rules, you truly start to live. Designing your life to have all the things that fill you up in it gives you ultimate freedom. And once you have that, there's always enough money.

Turns out, I wasn't the only person who had come to this conclusion. Bronnie Ware, an Australian author and palliative care nurse, discovered the same thing. In her book "The Top Five Regrets of the Dying: A Life Transformed by the Dearly Departing," she lists the following as the No. 1 regret:

"I wish I'd had the courage to live a life true to myself, not the life others expected of me." [31]

When I really think about it, I always knew this deep down in my core. And clearly, others knew and know it too!

The burden of my student loans and Wall Street had just temporarily corrupted me, as our experiences often do. My circumstances had led me to believe that there were no other options for me. I had fooled myself into believing that a cookie-cutter career and life were the way to success and happiness.

I clearly remember one morning after a Friday night out entertaining clients. Bob, for the first time ever, got to see the debauchery of Wall Street in action. And his girlfriend had been drunkity-drunk-drunk that night.

I remember waking up with him already awake and staring at me with a lot of worry in his eyes. "What?" I asked him. He lovingly touched my cheek and said: "I think you have a problem. Things were totally out of hand last night."

"What do you mean?" I asked, smiling at him (and thinking to myself, "this is totally freaking normal").

"Welcome to Wall Street. This is how we roll," I said. "It's just the way we do things, and besides, we're having so much fun."

I knew what I had just said was total bullshit. The truth is, we Wall Street types were adults in our 20s, 30s, 40s, and some 50s, who were partying it up like it was spring break every day. Lying, cheating, whoring, snorting.

This wasn't normal.

The people I was working with were using alcohol, drugs, and sex as an escape from their stressful and unfulfilling lives. That wasn't what I wanted for myself.

And I had always known this. My gut had been screaming at me for years. But, just like my colleagues, I was also numbing my inner wisdom with alcohol too.

Before I got corrupted by Wall Street's metric for success, I had always made decisions by asking myself: "If I got run over by a bus tomorrow, would I die happy? Would I have everything in my life that I wanted? Would I have done and accomplished everything that I wanted?"

So, after my sobering conversation with Bobby and taking stock of what my future held if I stayed on my current trajectory, I finally hit the eject button. On a cold morning in February 2009, right in the middle of the great recession, I walked into my boss' office and gave my career and its cushy salary the middle finger.

Turns out that being chained to a desk where you always had to eat your lunch hunched over a desk, while being interrupted 50 million times, where you couldn't go to the gym, where you were expected to entertain clients who treated you like a piece of meat but got paid loads of money—all of that felt like a dark, dingy prison cell. And it didn't bring me joy at all.

By that point, I had figured out that in order for me to be happy, I needed creative freedom, I needed flexibility in my schedule, and most importantly, I needed at least four weeks of vacation so I could visit my family in South Africa.

After leaving Wall Street, it took me two years to design my business and my life on my terms. It took commitment, and it took vision and believing in myself. I religiously worked, and continue to work, all the strategies I shared in this book.

I became a certified Pilates instructor who made my own schedule, and we ended up spending six weeks in South Africa in 2011. And we've done that almost every year since then.

Just like my old Wall Street self, you might have confined yourself to your own prison. And you might be justifying it by saying things like: "Well, this is the way you have to do it, because this is how others do it. You have to make sacrifices to be successful."

As a business owner, you might have started with the goal of freedom but ended up creating the exact opposite of it.

Maybe you're bogged down in the day-to-day, neglecting your health, sacrificing time with family and friends, pulling all-nighters, and only doing things related to your business. And you're doing it all in the name of someday making enough money to sell your business or to retire early.

As we saw in the previous chapter, when you do this, you become deeply dissatisfied and unhappy. But what if you got run over by a bus tomorrow?

Or what if your business never quite makes enough money for you to quit? (Remember, when you operate from a place of scarcity, no amount of money is ever going to be enough for you to walk away from it.)

Or perhaps your business is wildly successful—but will there be anyone left to celebrate with you?

In the documentary "Miss Americana," we see how hard the pop musician Taylor Swift works. She has an amazing work ethic, and for a long time, her entire life was consumed by her career. She pushed and pushed and pushed. And then when she finally won the award she had been dreaming of her whole life, she realized that there was no one to celebrate it with. She finally saw that all her sacrifices had left her with an award but not much else.

That moment so clearly reminded me of my own pursuit of success. In high school, it was all about studying to get better grades, ballet, music, my future career. It was all in service to the end result. And I was willing to forgo all the fun and beautiful moments that happened along the journey. Which made the journey lonely and terribly depressing.

This brings us to the rest of the regrets laid out in Bronnie Ware's book mentioned earlier:

1. *I wish I hadn't worked so hard.*
2. *I wish I'd had the courage to express my feelings.*
3. *I wish I had stayed in touch with my friends.*
4. *I wish that I had let myself be happier.*

At age 25, I already had all these feelings and thoughts. And when clients first start working with me, many of them also have one or more of these regrets.

Through our work together, I'm able to help them to intentionally design lives and businesses that bring them so much more joy and ease, and as a result, the money comes in abundance too.

Do you have any of the regrets Bronnie mentions?

It's time to set yourself free of all those remorseful feelings and realize everything you genuinely want for your business and your life.

This is your time to choose and prioritize your deepest desires, hopes, and dreams. And it all starts with you starting to think beyond the trappings of a traditional life.

It is your duty to identify all the possibilities for a richer existence that honors your unique needs and creative expression.

You now have all the tools and resources to step into that next dimension of what your life and business can and *deserves* to be.

Are you ready? Let's do this.

When I live life by my rules, I truly start to live.

Freedom is designing my life to have all the things in it that fill me up.

I set myself free of remorseful feelings and realize everything I truly want.

I choose and prioritize my deepest desires, hopes, and dreams.

UP LEVEL IT NOW:

1   *What's one regret that you have about your business or life (feel free to take one of Bronnie's if it resonates)? What actions can you take to rectify or rid yourself of this regret?*

2   *Where have you held yourself back by conforming to the norm?*

What do you really want? What actions can you take toward that goal now?

Don't forget to access your special book bonuses at the resource page, including an audio-recording of all the mantras in the "Make This Your Mantra" sections: hannekeantonelli.com/book-bonus

And we look forward to seeing you in the Up Level Program companion course: hannekeantonelli.com/up-level-project-program

EPILOGUE:

I thought this book was done

And then the coronavirus spread like a wildfire and turned the whole world upside down.

In that first week, when nearly everyone went into full-blown lockdown, it felt like we lived a million lives in one day.

I would be on the phone with a client helping them to come up with a plan in our one-hour session, and then two hours later, things would drastically change and we'd have to start all over again.

Just like you, my emotions have been all over the map. At times I've been confident about the future of my business and my ability to support existing clients and prospective ones. I've felt assured that I can be a leader. And the next moment, I doubt everything.

At one point, I even doubted coaching. All of a sudden my mind went into a tailspin. What if what I had to offer was complete and utter B.S.? What if all of it was just fluff that worked only when things were going well?

What if the cat was finally out of the bag? Was I a fraud?

And the worst part, I just wrote an entire freaking book about this work.

When you get paid for your intellectual property, it puts you in a very precarious place in a time of crisis. My "product" is the time I spend having a conversation with you. In that conversation, I help you come up with a solution or a new innovative business idea that's unique to you and where your business is. This idea will then help you to grow your business, make more money, expand your team, and run your company more efficiently.

And it was with that particular strategy in mind that I wrote this book. I wanted to ensure that when you were done reading it you'd stop listening to others' business opinions and you would level up and be the confident leader, and best CEO that you can be.

So I reflected on what I had written. And instantly, my confidence in my work and how I help business folks to weather this storm was restored.

It's then that I realized the only way through this crisis was by practicing my resiliency routine as if it were my business. In order to lead, inspire, and grow revenue, I would have to stay as grounded as possible. I'd have to stop looking to others to lead the way. I'd have to look within, practice self-leadership, and follow my business' specific road map out of this mess.

The only way forward was to listen to, and tap into, my gut, and most importantly get my beliefs, thoughts, words, feelings, and actions in alignment, and trust that I'd get the results I needed.

Immediately, what I needed to do came into focus. The way to lead, the way to support and hold space for my clients, the way to show up in the world, was all locked up in this book.

Coaching isn't bullshit. I have a special gift, a superpower in this moment of uncertainty that every business owner absolutely needs. My purpose right now is to show up and own it, and this book is an extension of my intention.

Now that you've read this book, you know that the way through this mess is to:

1. Make that commitment that you'll do whatever it takes to get through this

2. Get clear on your short-term strategy and long-term vision goals

3. And then evaluate, manage, and adjust the components of the Up Level Formula as if your life depended on it

Make your resiliency routine your top priority and act from a place of abundance instead of scarcity, which is so easy to focus on right now.

Yes, it might be chaotic. But by implementing the tools and strategies that you've gained in our journey together, you're now empowered to become a stronger and more confident leader.

It's your time to make the impossible happen.

And you don't have to do it alone. Remember: you can always join us in the next round of the Up Level Program, my online course that's a companion to this book.

You've got this. Now go get 'em!

ACKNOWLEDGMENTS:

Thank you to my husband, Bobby, for reminding me to have fun. Thank you for all your support and love throughout the whole book-writing process! And thank you for listening for countless hours as I obsessed over just about every detail about the book.

I'd like to thank my mom, who always modeled what it looked like to be a strong and independent woman. And thank you for being such a champion of all my crazy dreams, despite being thousands of miles away. And thanks to my brothers for your hand in raising a confident and brave lady.

Special thanks to all my clients who so graciously allowed me to share their testimonials and stories with you. Thank you for allowing me behind the scenes in your businesses—working with every one of you has been such a tremendous honor.

To James Reed, my friend and spectacular editor: I never imagined that writing a book would be this effortless and so much fun all at once. Thank you for making me a better writer, for pushing back on me, and for the many hours we spent on the phone and Zoom, and for all your time editing this book and ensuring that we produced something of outstanding quality. I can never thank you enough!

Thank you, Lisa McKenna, from Arrow North, LLC, for creating the most beautiful and on-brand cover and a beautiful book layout.

To personal stylist and my friend, Nicole Otchy, who helped pick a stunning outfit for the cover.

To Alma Bruffy of Alma B Photography, for taking the beautiful images for the book cover and author photo, and a few more for my website. And thank you for introducing me to makeup artist Jennifer Miller, who was so wonderful. Thank you both.

Thank you, Weaving Influence, for helping me get the word out about the book! Thank you particularly to Christy Kirk and Becky Robinson for all your help.

Thank you to Suzy Ashworth and Jack Pransky for allowing me to interview you for the book. (Remember, you can access those interviews via the book resources page: hannekeantonelli.com/book-bonus)

Thank you to my dear friend Steven Finch, mathematics wizard and research computing specialist at MIT Sloan School of Management, for your insights and help in establishing that the Up Level Formula is indeed a qualitative model.

Thank you to my coaches and mentors along the way, especially Shirley Scott, Denis O'Brien, and Tara Newman. You have all helped me so much.

Thank you to everyone who participated in being a book-launch team member. Your time helping to get the word out about the Up Level Project is much appreciated!

Thank you to my brother Daniël Hugo of Daniël Hugo Illustration for creating a beautiful brain image.

Thank you to every single friend and family member who, along the way, asked about the book and cheered me on. Your encouraging words kept me going!

NOTES:

CHAPTER 1: The Commitment: Going all in

1. Daniel K. Hall-Flavin, M.D., "Antidepressants can they stop working?" Jan. 31, 2018, Mayo Clinic, https://www.mayoclinic.org/diseases-conditions/depression/expert-answers/antidepressants/faq-20057938

2. Theodore Roosevelt, "The Man in the Arena," Apr. 23, 1910, https://www.theodorerooseveltcenter.org/Blog/Item/The%20Man%20in%20the%20Arena

3. Three Principles, Wikipedia, https://en.wikipedia.org/wiki/Three_Principles_(self-help)

CHAPTER 3: How to get what you really want

4. CPI Inflation Calculator, "Use Our Inflation Calculator," Feb. 10, 2021, https://www.in2013dollars.com/us/inflation

CHAPTER 5: Becoming friends with fear

5. Arash Javanbakht and Linda Saab, The Conversation, "What Happens in the Brain When We Feel Fear," Smithsonianmag.com, Oct. 27, 2017, https://www.smithsonianmag.com/science-nature/what-happens-brain-feel-fear-180966992/

6. Elizabeth Gilbert, "Big Magic", Aug. 21, 2015.

7. "World Population Review: Crime Rate by Country 2021," World Population Review, https://worldpopulationreview.com/countries/crime-rate-by-country/

8. Arash Javanbakht and Linda Saab, The Conversation, "What Happens in the Brain When We Feel Fear," Smithsonianmag.com, Oct. 27, 2017, https://www.smithsonianmag.com/science-nature/what-happens-brain-feel-fear-180966992/

9. Josh Pais, "Committed Impulse," https://committedimpulse.com/

CHAPTER 6: If only they had told us sooner

10. Jack Pransky, "Somebody Should Have Told Us! (Simple Truths for Living Well)," Jan. 10, 2006.

11. Danielle Reid, "Physical reaction definition and meaning," Study.com, Middle School Physical Science, Help and Review, Science Courses, Chapter 4 / Lesson 6, https://study.com/academy/lesson/physical-reaction-definition-examples.html

12. Neringa Antanaityte, "Mind Matters: How to Effortlessly Have More Positive Thoughts," TLEX Institute, https://tlexinstitute.com/how-to-effortlessly-have-more-positive-thoughts/#:~:text=In%202005%2C%20the%20National%20Science,thoughts%20as%20the%20day%20before.

13. Cecelia Health Marketing, "The Neuroscience of Behavior Change", Cecelia Health, Jun. 26, 2017, https://www.ceceliahealth.com/blog/2017/6/26/the-neuroscience-of-behavior-change

14. "What Is Tapping and How Can I Start Using It?," The Tapping Solution. https://www.thetappingsolution.com/what-is-eft-tapping/

CHAPTER 7: The beliefs that determine your success

15. Elana Lyn Gross, "How Tone It Up's Founders Created a Fitness Empire," Forbes, Aug. 14, 2017, https://www.forbes.com/sites/elanagross/2017/08/14/how-tone-it-ups-founders-created-a-fitness-empire/#35274a89723c

16. Jackelyn Ho, "How This Popular YouTuber Turned 4.1 Million Subscribers Into Diehard Customers," Inc., May 3, 2018, https://www.inc.com/jackelyn-ho/how-this-popular-youtuber-turned-41-million-subscribers-into-diehard-customers.html

17. Zumba, Wikipedia, https://en.wikipedia.org/wiki/Zumba

CHAPTER 8: Be sure to mind your language

18. Esther Hicks, Abraham Hicks, Abraham-Hicks Publications, https://www.abraham-hicks.com/

19. Don Miguel Ruiz, Janet Mills, "The Four Agreements: A Practical Guide to Personal Freedom," 1997

CHAPTER 9: Are you unknowingly sabotaging yourself?

20. Gay Hendricks, "The Big Leap: Conquer Your Hidden Fear and Take Life to the Next Level," Apr. 21, 2009.

CHAPTER 10: Feel it to achieve it and supercharge the Up Level Formula

21. Denise Duffield-Thomas, "Get Rich, Lucky Bitch!: Release Your Money Blocks and Live a First-Class Life," Apr. 19, 2013.

22. Abigail Brenner, "E~motions of Change = Energy in Motion," Psychology Today, Jun. 3, 2011, https://www.psychologytoday.com/us/blog/in-flux/201106/emotions-change-energy-in-motion

23. Pilar Gerasimo, "Emotional Biochemistry," Experience L!fe, Nov. 1, 2020, https://experiencelife.com/article/emotional-biochemistry/

CHAPTER 11: The one thing that will derail and delay your progress

24. Nancy Moyer, medically reviewed by Timothy J. Legg, "Amygdala Hijack: When Emotion Takes Over," Healthline, Apr. 22, 2019, https://www.health-line.com/health/stress/amygdala-hijack#overview

CHAPTER 13: A leader is born

25. Early life and career of Abraham Lincoln, Wikipedia, https://en.wikipedia.org/wiki/Early_life_and_career_of_Abraham_Lincoln

CHAPTER 15: Have a little faith… in yourself

26. Tama Kieves, "Inspired & Unstoppable: Wildly Succeeding in Your Life's Work!," Aug. 30, 2012.

CHAPTER 17: Speed up the upleveling process by stepping into the future

27. Dr. Jim Loehr, "The Only Way to Win," May 8, 2012.

CHAPTER 19: From lacking it all to having it all

28. Richard Dotts, "Dollars Flow to Me Easily," Jun. 14, 2016.

29. Denise Duffield-Thomas, "Get Rich, Lucky Bitch!: Release Your Money Blocks and Live a First-Class Life," Apr. 19, 2013.

30. Jen Sincero, "You Are a Badass at Making Money: Master the Mindset of Wealth," Apr. 18, 2017.

CHAPTER 20: Hello, success—and freedom!

31. Bronnie Ware, "The Top Five Regrets of the Dying: A Life Transformed by the Dearly Departing," Aug. 2019.

CPSIA information can be obtained
at www.ICGtesting.com
Printed in the USA
FSHW021433030421
80066FS